WRITING DOWN THE DRAGON

Books by Tom Simon

Lord Talon's Revenge

Death Carries a Camcorder and Other Essays

THE EYE OF THE MAKER
The End of Earth and Sky
The Grey Death (forthcoming)

Visit the author's website at
bondwine.com

WRITING DOWN
THE DRAGON
and Other Essays
on the Tolkien Method
and the Craft of Fantasy
by
TOM SIMON

Calgary
BONDWINE BOOKS
2013

Edited by Robin Eytchison
Cover design by Sarah Huntrods

Published by Bondwine Books
ISBN 978-0-9881292-5-2

TABLE OF CONTENTS

PREFACE

Slowly with the rolling years the obvious (so often the last revelation of analytic study) has been discovered: that we have to
deal with a poem by an Englishman using afresh ancient and
largely traditional material. At last then, after inquiring so long
whence this material came, and what its original or aboriginal
nature was (questions that cannot ever be decisively answered),
we might also now again inquire what the poet did with it. If we
ask that question, then there is still, perhaps, something lacking even in the major critics, the learned and revered masters
from whom we humbly derive.

—J. R. R. Tolkien, *'Beowulf: The Monsters and the Critics'*

This book is not written for experts; I have nothing to add to the
enormous chorus of voices already engaged in the business of
'Tolkien Studies'. If my observations have any value at all, it is
because I come at the matter from a different angle to most: as a *writer*
who has an especial interest in seeing what literary effects J. R. R. Tolkien was striving to create and how he produced them. He himself used
the metaphor of Story as a soup, in which many different ingredients
were boiled down until they lost their individual identity. For this reason, he said, it was of comparatively little use to inquire too deeply into

the things that went into the Pot; what really mattered was the Soup that came out of it.

As a reader, I have a good deal of sympathy with this view. As a lover of history and of interesting literary puzzles, I have some sympathy even with the source critics. But as a writer, I want to examine Tolkien's bag of professional tricks; I want to know his art of cookery. And I am writing this monograph on the subject, not because I think I have any definitive answers, but because I am deeply interested in the questions, and want to share my thoughts with others who may share the same interest and have insights of their own.

For after we have done with all the critics, both the source critics who seek the ingredients that went into the Pot, and the textual critics who judge the qualities of the Soup, we are left with a Cook. To borrow Tolkien's own words: Slowly with the rolling years, the obvious has been discovered: that we have to deal with a cycle of stories by an Englishman using afresh ancient and largely traditional material. At last then, after inquiring so long whence this material came, we might also now again inquire what the storyteller did with it, *and how he did it.* That is the study I want to pursue in more detail; and if my pursuit leaves learned folk bored, bemused, or angry, I beg their indulgence. This book is not for the Wise, but for my fellow beginners in the craft of Fantasy, who are trying to learn some of the master's techniques and want to compare notes.

THE RIDDLES OF THE WISE

Of this two things are said, though which is true only those
Wise could say who now are gone.

> —J. R. R. Tolkien, *Unfinished Tales
> of Númenor and Middle-earth*

As Tolkien observed, the obvious is often the last thing revealed
by analytic study. If only for the sake of novelty, then, let us
begin with the obvious and work from there. The obvious thing
about Tolkien – the thing he insisted on to everyone who would listen –
was that his stories were 'primarily linguistic in inspiration'. Many students of Tolkien seem baffled or even offended by this, and take great
trouble to deny that he meant what he said. Certainly it is not the usual
way to write fiction; but it is by no means impossible, and Tolkien, of
all writers, grew up in the circumstances most calculated to give him a
linguist's view of literature.

To begin with, he was exposed as a child to a remarkable variety of
languages. The linguists tell us that a child's first experience of language
will colour his way of speaking and thinking for life; in particular, a child
brought up with more than one language will very probably acquire the
knack that people call 'a gift for languages'. Tolkien spent his earliest years
in South Africa, often in the care of servants. There he began to learn

English, of course; but he was also exposed to Afrikaans and to one or more of the Bantu languages: that is, a language closely related to English, and a language-group completely unrelated and obviously alien. In England he was exposed to the different dialects of city and country, the middle class and the (rapidly vanishing) West Midlands peasantry, as well as the exotic Welsh names on coal-trains. At school, as a matter of course, he was taught Latin, Greek, and (much less thoroughly) French; and after his mother's conversion to Catholicism he began to learn Spanish from her priest, Fr. Francis Morgan, who became his guardian after her premature death. That makes at least eight languages to go on with. And then there were the Pan-Teutonists.

The early twentieth century was above all others the age of 'scientific' racism, and particularly of a virulent inter-white bigotry, now almost forgotten. The fact, for instance, that Englishmen had long heads and Poles had wide heads was thought to be of immense biological significance. In Europe there was comparatively little talk of 'the white race'; it was subdivided into at least five subraces – Teutons, Celts, 'Latins', Slavs, and Jews – and each subrace had its contingent of crazy academics who seriously claimed its absolute superiority over the rest. Pan-Teutonism began as a political movement to reunite the numerous small states of Germany, but it soon took on racial and racist overtones, and by 1900 the Pan-Teutonists were preaching a kind of mystical brotherhood of all the peoples who spoke Germanic languages – and, of course, the categorical inferiority of everyone else.

Terminology is sometimes fatal. It was an Anglo-Welsh philologist, Sir William Jones, who first suggested that most of the languages of Europe and North India were descended from a single ancestor, now lost. But it was at the German universities of the nineteenth century that Indo-European studies really caught on. The Germans, however, did not call the language group Indo-European, but *Indogermanisch* – giving short shrift to languages from Latin to Persian. They became rather fixated on the alleged common descent of the Germanic peoples and the Aryans, an assumption that became one of the characteristic insanities of the age. It was because of their linguistic work that the term *Aryan* came to be misapplied to the Germans and kindred nations. The consequences of that were followed with brutal, if cockeyed, logic down to their conclusion in the *Götterdämmerung* of the Second World War, when a mad Austrian tramp led Germany to destruction under a flag based on a Hindu religious symbol.

The racism of the Pan-Teutonists never appealed to Tolkien, who admired the Jews and called Hitler a 'ruddy little ignoramus'. But in his youth before the World Wars, it was easy to take up a *linguistic* interest in Germanic studies – much easier than it is now, when philology has virtually disappeared from the university curricula of the English-speaking countries. You could immerse yourself in Norse mythology and Wagnerian opera, Old English and Icelandic and Gothic, in a kind of ecstatic innocence, not imagining that the world-view of the ancient Teutons would one day become an excuse for a universal bloodbath. And that is what Tolkien did. In the course of these studies he also had to develop a thorough working knowledge of modern German, since most philological papers were published in that language. When he took up his romantic desire to invent a language of his own, it was only natural that he should think of an 'unrecorded' Germanic tongue.

For Tolkien was also a romantic, and a frustrated storyteller. Every Tolkienist knows how, as a child of seven, Tolkien tried to write a story about a dragon. He described it as 'a green great dragon', and was mightily puzzled when his mother told him he had to say *great green dragon* instead. ('I wondered why, and still do,' he wrote to W. H. Auden many years later.) In boyhood he often played at inventing nonsensical languages like 'Animalic' and 'Nevbosh'; as an undergraduate he tried his hand at what we may call a *sensical* language. He had read Joseph Wright's Gothic grammar, and as much other Gothic material as he could get his hands on, and was moved and inspired by the tragic history of the Goths. At this stage, it appears, he wanted to invent a Germanic tribe of his own, whose language would *be* its history – much as the history of the pre-Roman Britons survives to a considerable extent in the cryptic evidence of place-names.

By this time Tolkien was properly trained in all the professional techniques of the philologist, with an especial nose for 'cruxes'. In philology, a crux is a plain corruption in a text, or a contradiction between two versions of a text, from which at first sight it seems impossible to recover the author's original meaning. This is the kind of puzzle that calls forth all a philologist's powers, and Tolkien delighted in solving them, or at least proposing ingenious and original solutions which might or might not stand up to further scrutiny. A similar kind of puzzle occurs when two languages with a common (but unwritten) ancestor have two forms of a word that are obviously related, but the different forms are not accounted for by the known laws of linguistic change. This kind of evidence can be invaluable in helping to reconstruct the history of a language and its speakers. Sometimes, however, the evidence is so sparse and ambiguous that competing theories can survive side by side for decades, waiting for new data to decide in favour of one or the other. This is notoriously the case with early Germanic.

In the nineteenth century, linguists divided the Germanic languages into three subgroups: North Germanic (the Scandinavian languages), East Germanic (Gothic), and West Germanic (German, Dutch, Frisian, and English). It was then generally supposed that languages were subject to something like the laws of heredity, and that a new language, like a new species, evolved from a single identifiable ancestor in a simple and orderly way: this was called the *Stammbaum* or 'family tree' model. *Homo habilis* begat *Homo erectus,* which begat *Homo neanderthalensis;* in the same way, Primitive Germanic begat Gothic, Old West Germanic, and Old North Germanic. But which came first? One theory held that Gothic became separate from 'Common Germanic' at an early date, and the Western and Northern branches split apart later. Another theory had West Germanic splitting off first, and North Germanic giving rise to Gothic separately.

This kind of simplistic branching model is out of favour today, and in fact there is strong evidence against it. What usually happens is that particular words, or particular tricks of grammar, spread in particular geographic areas, but each in its own time and its own way. Modern linguists construct elaborate maps of these variations, which generally show a pattern of gradual change from one district to another. Mark Twain made at least one linguistic observation of this kind. He noted that in the United States in his time, Southerners tended to use *went* as a past participle instead of *gone,* and Northerners used the nonstandard expression *hadn't ought.* One day he heard a man say, 'He hadn't ought to have went,' and instantly 'placed' him as a hybrid – one parent Northern, the other Southern. But there might have been a district (in Kentucky or Maryland, say) where the two usages naturally overlapped.

This idea of overlapping dialects was beginning to catch on in Tolkien's youth, and the whole picture of Primitive Germanic was consequently in flux. It appeared that in some ways, English and Frisian were closer to the Scandinavian languages than they were to German; and German itself was a fusion of many different dialects which had their separate origins in remote antiquity. The whole idea of 'West Germanic' and 'North Germanic' was beginning to come into question.

Another picture began to emerge; Tolkien was at least aware of it, and may have favoured it over the standard interpretation. Languages diverge because different groups of speakers have little contact with one another; conversely, languages hold together or converge when their speakers can easily travel and trade together. In the days of the later Roman Empire, the Germanic-speaking countries could be roughly divided into four distinct regions. The North Sea coast formed one region, where the influence of Frisian traders kept the local dialects in regular contact. The upper Danube basin roughly defined another region, where Roman influence was strongest, and Germans of many tribes served together as auxiliaries in the Roman army; this, too, tended to keep their dialects from diverging too far. Away to the east, the Goths and related tribes lived a semi-nomadic life on the Ukrainian steppes, and developed their language in their own way without much influence from the other Germans. In the middle was a group that the Romans called *Istvaeones,* the ancestors of the Franks, Flemish, and Dutch, among others. From about AD 200 on, the Scandinavians began to constitute a fifth dialect-group; whether it split off from the North Sea group, or from early Gothic, or evolved in parallel with them from Primitive Germanic, is a moot point among Germanists. The North Sea Germans were called *Ingvaeones* by the Romans – the People of Yngvi.

It is here that we cross from philology into mythology. There was a rather snide saying among one school of linguists, that 'mythology is a disease of language'; to which Tolkien retorted that European languages, at any rate, were diseases of mythology. Yngvi was the mythical ancestor of the North Sea tribes, the 'worshipper of Ing'. Ing seems to have been the proper name of the Germanic god Freyr – the latter name simply means 'lord'. Yngvi was one of the three sons of Mannus ('Man') in early Germanic legend. Mannus and his sons were taken up into the Germanic religion as gods, or at any rate demigods, along with such other mysterious and possibly historical figures as Scef (or Sheave) and Scyld Scefing – who may have been an ancestor of the present British royal family. Yngvi also occurs as the legendary ancestor of the Ynglings, the earliest Swedish royal family; this may not be the same Yngvi who was the son of Mannus, but at minimum, the coincidence of names shows a close cultural link between the North Sea tribes and the Scandinavians.

All this linguistic matter, and the myths that were interwoven with it, worked powerfully on the young Tolkien's imagination. He had been particularly interested in the problem of the elves in Norse myth. The surviving body of Norse (and Old English) legend contains no actual *stories* about elves, but a surprising amount of detail about their ethnic divisions – information that was thought important enough to preserve, though the reasons for preserving it are lost. When he began writing his 'Book of Lost Tales' or 'History of the Elves', Tolkien divided his *Qendi* into three kindreds, loosely recalling the division of the Norse *álfar* into *ljósálfar, dökkálfar,* and *svartálfar.* Then, borrowing from one legend to explain another – this would become one of his most characteristic tricks – he wrote how each kindred of the *Qendi* was founded by a famous king. The noblest kindred of all was the *Teleri,* whose king was called *Inwë* or *Ing* – a clear echo of the Germanic names. (Finwë Nólemë and Tinwë Linto, the other two kings in the earliest stories, would in this analogy correspond to Irmin and Istaev, the other sons of Mannus.) But by inventing Inwë/Ing, Tolkien was creating a crux of his own: How did these two different names come to be applied to the same person? The solution to this crux gives a potent key to the Tolkien method.

Not long after Tolkien began work on his invented Germanic language, he discovered the *Kalevala* in W. F. Kirby's English translation, and was delighted by it. This was a new flavour of legend, sharply different from either the Greek myths he had read in school or the Norse myths of his philological studies. It bore a striking resemblance to the folklore of the North American natives, whom Englishmen of his generation still called 'Red Indians'. (Indeed, when Longfellow compiled and adapted various Ojibwe legends into *The Song of Hiawatha,* he wrote his poem in a deliberate pastiche of the *Kalevala* metre.) Tolkien had read James Fenimore Cooper as a boy, and keenly felt the romantic appeal of virgin forests, bows and arrows, and things of that kind. The *Kalevala* gave him all that, and to top off the feast, a language quite outside the Indo-European family, with a structure and music all of its own.

His discovery of Finnish made him throw his original ambition to the winds. Instead of an unrecorded Germanic dialect, Tolkien began work on a family of languages, one patterned after Finnish, another recalling the sound and style of Welsh, but both connected by a common ancestry and root vocabulary. The Finnish-flavoured language he called *Qenya,* and the Welsh-flavoured one 'Gnomish'; he made these the tongues of two of his Elvish peoples, and postulated a 'Primitive Eldarin' that was the ancestor of both. (He also sketched in a large but constantly varying set of cognate languages, never worked out in any detail, from which he could draw particular words when he wanted to break the rules he had set for Qenya and Gnomish.) It was easy to resolve the Yngvi/Ing crux in this new model: *Inwë* (later *Ingwë*) was the Qenya form, *Ing* the Gnomish.

(I should point out that in a later development of the *Lost Tales,* Tolkien explicitly introduced the Germanic legend of Yngvi/Ing into the conclusion of the work; but this never proceeded beyond rough jottings and outlines. It would in any case have been unspeakably confusing to have both Inwë/Ing, the Elvish king, and Yngvi/Ing, the Germanic king, in the same tale.)

By now, Tolkien was in full-scale reaction against his original intentions. He deliberately chose not to relate his invented languages to any linguistic family in the real world: a decision that fit perfectly with the idea that the speakers were not humans at all, but various kinds of elves. This meant that he had to reinvent most of the basic vocabulary: a large task, but one that gave his sense of linguistic aesthetics free play. He could devise Qenya and Gnomish words and grammar purely to please his own ear, unconstrained by any existing language.

This is not to say that he did not borrow (or retain) individual words from real languages. As a boy, he had read a book that claimed (among other odd things) that only two words were now known from the language of the pre-Celtic inhabitants of Britain. One of those words stuck in his mind: *ond,* meaning 'stone'. He liked the sound of it, and since he designed his languages to include the sounds he liked best, it fitted in easily as a Qenya word. The Gnomish equivalent, by the phonetic laws he had invented, would be *gond.* In the 'Lost Tales', the last city of the Gnomes to hold out against the evil of Melko was accordingly called *Gondolin,* 'the Stone of Song'; and 'The Fall of Gondolin' was the first story to be completed. In later years, when the whole history of the Elvish languages had been changed, and the languages themselves heavily refined, the name *Gondolin* posed another crux: it no longer fit the morphology of Sindarin (which had evolved out of the earlier Gnomish). So Tolkien made up another dialect for the people of Gondolin, a mixture of Quenya and Sindarin spoken nowhere else. While writing *The Lord of the Rings* he invented 'the Land of Ond', the last redoubt of the exiled Men of Númenor; but then he decided that all the place-names of that region should be Sindarin in form, so he renamed it Gondor.

Ond was not the only word that Tolkien filched for his own use. There was also the Greek word *gorgos,* 'terrible', which we know from the myth of the Gorgons – Medusa and her sisters. This word itself is a bit of a puzzle. It seems to have cognates in Old Irish and Armenian, but then again it may come from a non-Indo-European source; as always when evidence is scarce, the theories vary freely. Tolkien appears to have adapted it into Gnomish as *gorgor,* which he made out to be an intensified form of *gor,* also meaning 'terrible'. This word occurs in the *Silmarillion* in the name *Ered Gorgoroth* 'Mountains of Terror', and in *The Lord of the Rings* in *Cirith Gorgor,* the pass into Mordor where the Black Gate was built, and *Gorgoroth,* the ash-choked desert around Mount Doom. Again there is the Irish *nasc* 'ring', which Tolkien acknowledged as the probable source of *nazg,* the word for 'ring' in the Black Speech. This word, too, is a bit of an oddity, being (as Tolkien said) a 'short, hard, and clear vocable' that does not particularly fit the style of 'a mushy language' like Gaelic.

Sometimes Tolkien would fasten on a 'crux' that existed only in the fevered imaginations of humourless and pretentious philologists. Such a case gave rise to the hobbit-song, *There is an inn, a merry old inn,* which Frodo sang at Bree. The nursery rhyme 'Hey Diddle Diddle' was the subject of a surprisingly hot academic dispute in Victorian times, derived entirely from the supposition that every word in a poem *must* have originally had a definite and serious meaning. What on earth, then, does 'hey diddle diddle' mean? Theory after theory was advanced and shot down, culminating in the wild idea that the apparent nonsense-syllables were a corrupt form of a Greek phrase. It remained for Tolkien to prick the balloon of philological pomposity by reminding his colleagues once more of the obvious: sometimes a nonsense phrase really *is* nonsense. He recast the first couplet:

> *So the cat on the fiddle played hey-diddle-diddle,*
> *a jig that would wake the dead;*

– making it obvious that the mysterious words merely represent the sound of a fiddle being played very fast. Tolkien dressed up this 'discovery' with the playful assertion that his poem was the lost original from which the nursery rhyme derived, but 'Only a few words of it are now, as a rule, remembered'. The entire exercise was a magnificent burlesque of the philological method, arriving at the obvious conclusion with an anticlimactic bump.

Sometimes Tolkien would manufacture a crux out of sheer aesthetic outrage. In his famous letter to Auden, Tolkien wrote of his 'bitter disappointment and disgust' at 'the shabby use made in Shakespeare of the coming of "Great Birnam wood to high Dunsinane hill": I longed to devise a setting in which the trees might really march to war.' Out of this, and a mysteriously evocative line from the Anglo-Saxon poem *The Wanderer* –

> *Eald enta geweorc idlu stodon*
> ('The old works of giants stood desolate')

– he devised the Ents and their role in *The Lord of the Rings*. The 'crux', if it may be so called, was that (in Tolkien's view) the fulfilment of the prophecy in *Macbeth* was no fulfilment at all; clearly this was a corruption introduced by an incompetent scribe, or in more literal terms, the error of an insufficiently imaginative playwright. When the Ents led the Huorns up to the gates of Helm's Deep, they were merely doing what *should* have happened at Dunsinane. The wood really did come to the high hill and win the battle.

Of course Tolkien knew he was playing a game with these cruxes, real or imagined, and in a way a rather childish game. It may have been partly as a sendup of his own professional methods that he wrote, in the Prologue of *The Lord of the Rings*:

> The genealogical trees at the end of the Red Book of Westmarch are a small book in themselves, and all but Hobbits would find them exceedingly dull. Hobbits delighted in such things, if they were accurate: they liked to have books filled with things they already knew, set out fair and square with no contradictions.

When Tolkien came up with an imaginative way of equating Yngvi with Ing, or making Birnam Wood really march to war as the prophecy foretold, he was using the tools of philology to resolve 'contradictions' so that the results could be 'set out fair and square'. It was one of his chief delights, and added much depth to his work. A third-rate philologist sees a contradiction between two versions of a text, and tries to make up his mind which one is accurate and which one is corrupt. A first-rate philologist tries to reconstruct the original in such a way as to account for *both* versions. Tolkien, by this standard, was a first-rate philologist. But the real fun would begin when he applied the tools of philology to his own manuscripts.

THE TOLKIEN METHOD

There are, I suppose, always defects in any large-scale work of art; and especially in those of literary form that are founded on an earlier matter which is put to new uses.... In which class, as a class not as a competitor, *The Lord of the Rings* really falls though it is only founded on the author's own first draft!
—*The Letters of J. R. R. Tolkien*, no. 156 (to Robert Murray)

Three removes are as bad as a fire.
—Benjamin Franklin, *Poor Richard's Almanack*

If Tolkien's house-moves were as disruptive as Franklin's (or my own) – and we have evidence from his letters that they were – the first great discontinuity in the history of Middle-earth will come as no surprise. In 1920 he moved from Oxford to Leeds to take the post of Reader in English Language; and just about that time he definitely abandoned work on the *Lost Tales*. It may be that the notebooks containing the original manuscripts were packed up for some time after the move, so that if Tolkien wanted to pursue the 'Matter' of Middle-earth further, he had to make a fresh start and work partly from memory. At Leeds he wrote an enormously long (but incomplete) 'Lay of the Children of Húrin' in alliterative verse. This poem shows throughout that he still had a vivid and exact recollection of the *Lost Tales,* but it moves beyond them in several important respects. In particular, the Elvish city of Nargothrond is here first developed and described. In 1925 he began work on another long poem, the 'Lay of Leithian' in rhyming couplets; and in that year, quite unexpectedly, he moved again.

It was in 1925 that W. A. Craigie, the professor of Anglo-Saxon at Oxford, resigned to take a position at the University of Chicago. Tolkien applied for the vacant chair, not with much hope, for at thirty-three he was still rather a junior scholar. To his surprise, he was accepted, and had to move back to Oxford. This time he definitely lost important threads of his hobby. He never again resumed work on the Húrin poem, or even told his sons about it, and with one exception his later works make no direct reference to the *Lost Tales.*

He did, however, show the Húrin poem to R. W. Reynolds, for whom he composed a 'Sketch of the mythology' in 1926. This was not exactly a summary of the *Lost Tales.* For one thing, Tolkien wrote it from memory, apparently without referring to the original texts. It also contains a number of elements not found in the *Lost Tales* at all, or even in the projected revision. All Tolkien's subsequent work on *The Silmarillion* follows on from the 'Sketch', except for the creation-myth, the *Ainulindalë,* which is taken directly from the *Lost Tales.* The *Ainulindalë* had to be revised so that it would match the later *Silmarillion* text, but this was largely a matter of correcting those names that Tolkien had changed. By that time, this was the least of his difficulties with his own texts.

For it is here that we begin to see the most interesting feature of the Tolkien method. Up to this time he had generally worked within a single 'tradition', as a philologist might put it: one definite line of manuscripts, proceeding from a first draft (usually in pencil) to a second draft (written over top of the first in ink) and then to later corrections and rewritings. Already in the *Lost Tales* the revised texts formed a fearsome maze, with bits of the same story spread across several notebooks, sometimes right in the middle of other stories – for Tolkien had little money to spend on paper, and when a revision turned out longer than the original manuscript, he had to put the excess wherever he could find room. It must have taken a remarkably tenacious and organized memory for him to keep track of these notebooks even for his own use. By the early 1930s, when the 'Sketch' had been developed into a book called the *Quenta Noldor-inwa*, the complexity of the manuscripts began to outrun even Tolkien's powers of organization.

In the 1930s, there appeared a third and even a fourth tradition. The third tradition began, famously, with Tolkien scribbling on a blank page of an examination booklet, 'In a hole in the ground there lived a hobbit.' It is not too much to say that this scrap of manuscript posed a 'crux' that Tolkien would spend the rest of his life unravelling. It did not, at first, seem to fit into the world that contained Gondolin and the Silmarils; but it was drawn in, irresistibly, and had to be made to fit. Tolkien filched names and motifs from one work to use in the other. So *The Hobbit* contained references to Gondolin and Elrond, and (as John D. Rateliff has shown) the description of the Arkenstone was later reused to describe the Silmarils. The fourth tradition began with Tolkien's recurring dreams about the fall of Atlantis, the gigantic blue wave rolling inexorably over field and forest and mountain. After a youthful fling as a time-travel story called *The Lost Road*, it settled down to a productive life as the legend of Númenor. It became clear that *The Hobbit* was set in a much later period of history than *The Silmarillion;* the Atlantis-story had to come in between. So the Second and Third Ages of Middle-earth came into being.

To reconcile all these stories, to make the whole history unified and self-consistent, taxed Tolkien's skills to the limit. The problem became urgent when he began writing *The Lord of the Rings,* for it was then that he first seriously began to weave all the threads into a single tapestry. You could say that the story of Sauron and the One Ring was a sequel to *The Silmarillion;* the story of Aragorn and Gondor, a sequel to *The Lost Road;* and the story of Frodo and Sam, a sequel to *The Hobbit.* Now each of those older stories had to be treated philologically, as a source manuscript of variable quality and reliability, and the differences between them had to be ironed out. Tolkien still had (and exploited) considerable freedom to rewrite or ignore bits of *The Silmarillion* and *The Lost Road* that did not suit his needs; but in *The Hobbit* he had to deal with a 'privileged' manuscript – a finished book, published and therefore unchangeable.

Or so he thought. In the original version of *The Hobbit,* Gollum is a rather more pathetic and less menacing character; he actually offers to bet his ring against Bilbo's life in the riddle-game. Once Tolkien fastened on the idea that Bilbo's ring was in fact the One Ring, this obviously would not do. Gollum would never even pretend to bet or barter it. How, then, to account for the story? If the Ring was so important – so *addictive* – that its bearer could not let it go, then Bilbo's tale must be a lie, a self-justifying fiction to give him some kind of lawful claim. So Tolkien put an alternative account into the Prologue of *The Lord of the Rings,* with the explanation:

> Now it is a curious fact that this is not the story as Bilbo first told it to his companions. To them his account was that Gollum had promised to give him a *present,* if he won the game; but when Gollum went to fetch it from his island he found the treasure was gone: a magic ring, which had been given to him long ago on his birthday. Bilbo guessed that this was the very ring that he had found, and as he had won the game, it was already his by right. But being in a tight place, he said nothing about it, and made Gollum show him the way out, as a reward instead of a present. This account Bilbo set down in his memoirs, and he seems never to have altered it himself, not even after the Council of Elrond.

Then, purely as 'a specimen of re-writing', he revised Chapter 5 of *The Hobbit* to incorporate the revised version of the Gollum story. He sent this to Stanley Unwin in 1947, and had evidently forgotten all about it when it very suddenly appeared in print three years later, in a new edition of *The Hobbit.* After that, Tolkien had to take into account both versions of the story, and explain how they came to exist side by side. So he wrote in the Prologue, referring again to the old version of the Gollum story:

Evidently it still appeared in the original Red Book, as it did in several of the copies and abstracts.

These 'copies and abstracts', then, would be the (fictitious) sources for the original *Hobbit* text. Meanwhile, the *motive* for Bilbo's lie – that the Ring was already beginning to corrupt his mind, as it had corrupted Gollum's – powerfully informed the second half of the sequel. It was that addictive power that made Frodo a shadow of himself, who had to be carried on Sam's shoulders up the slopes of Mount Doom; and it determined the whole tragic character of Gollum as finally developed. Tolkien had solved his self-imposed 'crux' brilliantly, and the solution gave him one of the most powerful and original elements in *The Lord of the Rings*.

That set a pattern, and it is a characteristic pattern in Tolkien's later work. It became his rule, whenever he set out to revise an old manuscript, to begin by making two typescript copies, one to edit, one for safekeeping in his files; but he could never keep straight which was the archive copy. He developed a disconcerting habit of making contradictory alterations on *both* copies. Then the differences became cruxes themselves, and had to be reconciled and synthesized into a single finished tale; for he usually found, when this happened, that both versions contained new ideas that he liked and wanted to keep.

Sometimes, indeed, one version had to be 'privileged' over the other. For instance, when Tolkien revised *The Lord of the Rings* in 1965–66, to prepare a new edition that would be subject to U.S. copyright, he had a free hand to change the text but not the map. The first edition had been meticulously correct in all its descriptions of places and distances, but it was based on his own map, made in coloured chalks in 1943 and therefore too expensive to reproduce in print. It was his son Christopher's redrawn map that was printed in the books, and of course it contained numerous small changes and errors. So Tolkien meticulously revised every passage where the text conflicted with Christopher's map, treating the map as definitive.

After *The Lord of the Rings* was published, Tolkien had another creative burst full of new material on the Third Age. He spent enormous time and energy responding to questions from readers, and significantly developed bits of the legendarium that were obscure in the published work. To one reader he explained a crux in his own texts: Hobbits *give* presents on their birthdays, but Gollum (who was a Hobbit himself) *received* the Ring on his birthday, and called it his birthday-present to justify his possession of it. To resolve this, he wound up answering the reader with a long letter on the folkways and what we might call the anthropology of Hobbits, ranging far beyond the original question.

Both during and after the composition of *The Lord of the Rings,* Tolkien frequently resorted to his trick of using one puzzle in his work as the solution to another. The greatest mystery of all in *The Hobbit* – greater even than Bilbo's ring – was the meaning of the word *hobbit* itself. Having followed Bilbo's adventures so far, we knew a good deal about the capacities and folkways of Hobbits, but next to nothing about their history, and nothing at all about the origin of their curious name.

Outside the story, he was aware that he had been influenced by traditional names for house-sprites and hobgoblins, of which 'Hobberdy Dick' is a fairly typical example – though Tolkien seems not to have heard of that particular name when he made up *hobbit*. He was more influenced by Sinclair Lewis's *Babbitt*: the smug bourgeois quality of the Hobbits, their obsession with 'respectability', their willingness to judge things they had never seen based on the painfully few things they had seen – all this element was strongly informed by his reading of Lewis's great Modernist novel. It would be too much to say that Sinclair Lewis *inspired* that side of the Hobbits; as a solidly middle-class Englishman, Tolkien hardly needed an American model from which to draw the idea of bourgeois respectability. But the *name* appealed to him, the sound of the word itself; like *ond* and *gorgos,* it perfectly answered his aesthetic and imaginative needs, and only wanted a bit of adaptation – what writers nowadays like to call 'filing off the serial numbers'. (The name *Babbitt* appealed to a lot of people in that way. 'Babbitry' was one of H. L. Mencken's favourite terms of abuse, and both *babbitt* and *babbitry* quickly made their way into English dictionaries.) Roughly speaking, you could say that Hobberdy Dick, the homely but puckish sprite of the English countryside, supplied the first syllable of *hobbit*, and Babbitt supplied the second. One appeared in Bilbo as his 'Tookish side', the other made him a solid respectable Baggins. 'Adventures! Nasty uncomfortable things! Make you late for dinner!' Together they made the Hobbit that sadly representative modern type, the cultural hybrid who has forgotten both sides of his ancestry, and in consequence does not even know himself.

But none of this helped Tolkien come up with an explanation of the name *inside* the story. That had to wait until his sudden discovery of Rohan. In a way, the Rohirrim were the long-delayed fruition of his old desire to invent a fictitious Germanic tribe. In their history and geography, the Riders of Rohan correspond loosely to the Goths; like them, they were great horsemen and steppe-dwellers, and received a large and attractive grant of territory from an older civilized nation to the south. The Men of Rohan got their country as a gift from the failing power of Gondor, in exchange for an alliance. The Goths received Dacia from the Romans in a similar fashion – though the alliance did not last, and the relationship between the Goths and Romans turned out tragically for both sides. But in language and culture, the Rohirrim rather resemble the men of Mercia from whom Tolkien (on his mother's side) was himself descended. Even their name for their own country, 'the Mark', is taken directly from Old Mercian: the name *Mercia* is just a Latinized version of *Mark*.

Since the Rohirrim were an 'unrecorded' Germanic people, their language and history could easily be fitted in with those of the Hobbits, otherwise so exogenous and unexplained. The idea had already developed that Gollum, or Sméagol, was originally a Hobbit, whose people dwelt in the valley of the upper Anduin. It was an easy matter to have Eorl the Young ride down out of the same region to lead his people into Rohan; easy and utterly logical.

The rest could be patterned on the *Völkerwanderung*, the Great Migration of the Germanic peoples in late antiquity. If the Rohirrim had migrated south like the Goths, the Hobbits could have migrated west like the English. That story was taken straight out of the earliest legendary incidents in English history. The Hobbits had three kindreds – the Stoors, Harfoots, and Fallohides; the Stoors were marsh-dwellers both in their old country by the Anduin and in their new land, the Shire; the Fallohides were less numerous, but more adventurous, and tended to take the lead in any new enterprise. The Germanic peoples who went to Britain also had three kindreds, the Angles, Saxons, and Jutes; the Angles were so named after the rather marshy region they once occupied, in what is now Schleswig-Holstein; the Jutes were less numerous but more adventurous, and were the first to make the jump to the island of Britain. The Shire was founded by two Fallohide brothers, Marcho and Blanco; the first Anglo-Saxon kingdom in Britain, Kent, was founded by two Jute brothers, Hengest and Horsa. All four names, Marcho, Blanco, Hengest, and Horsa, are technical or poetic terms from Old English meaning 'horse'.

So the Hobbits, upon reflection or 'retconning', became another unrecorded Germanic people, or rather, a people whose language could be represented in Germanic terms. That meant that the Rohirrim, unlike most other Men, would have some memory of Hobbits, on the level of folktale. It also accounted for the close similarity between the language of Rohan and that of the Shire, especially in the matter of place-names. Above all, it provided a ready-made etymology for the word *hobbit* itself. It was an easy matter for Tolkien to find a suitable etymon: *hol-bytla,* an unrecorded but perfectly valid Old English compound word meaning 'hole-dweller'. The original mystery, which Tolkien had created with his one scribbled sentence, was solved with exquisite neatness. Of course 'in a hole in the ground there lived in a hobbit': that is what *hobbit* means.

This impulse to explain and tie different stories together, as I have said, continued for many years after *The Lord of the Rings* was published. One of the best instances in Tolkien's late work is the tale of Queen Berúthiel. While composing *The Lord of the Rings,* he made Aragorn say this about Gandalf: 'He is surer of finding the way home in a blind night than the cats of Queen Berúthiel.' It was intended as a throwaway remark, a reference to a bit of folklore that did not actually exist: a common trick used by many writers, not just of fantasy, to make their invented worlds seem larger than the actual story. Naturally enough, Tolkien came to be pestered by fans who wanted to know all about Queen Berúthiel; and eventually he made up a story to go with the name. Characteristically, he used this mystery to solve another – the first great civil war in Gondor, referred to in the Appendices of *The Lord of the Rings,* which came from the disputed succession after King Tarannon died childless. Why was Tarannon childless, if having a clear heir was so vitally important in Gondorian politics? The answer, Tolkien decided, was that he had a foreign wife of a peculiarly horrible sort, whom he had married for reasons of state but could get no children by: Queen Berúthiel. She was what we should describe as a witch or sorceress, and the cats, in effect, were her familiars, which she used to spy on the people of Gondor – until the King and the nation alike got fed up with her, and packed her aboard a ship to send her back to her own country. He even provided a good Quenya etymology for the name *Berúthiel,* which perfectly suited the Queen's character. By tying these two previously unexplained 'bits' together, Tolkien explained them both, and in so doing, made Middle-earth seem larger and more real than it did before.

Unfortunately, the greatest crux, or series of cruxes, exceeded even Tolkien's powers to reconcile. That was the business of working out all the variant texts and riders of the *Silmarillion* manuscripts into a coherent whole, consistent with itself and with the published *Lord of the Rings.* In his last years, he wrote some very interesting essays on matters arising from *The Silmarillion,* and recast several of the major stories in bold new ways; these (unfinished) manuscripts are among his best writing, though, in the event, it proved impossible to include them all in the published *Silmarillion.* A typical piece of this type is 'Of Tuor and His Coming to Gondolin', a fragment of rewriting which, if finished, would have completely recast the old tale of 'The Fall of Gondolin'. So far as it goes, it is one of his best pieces of writing: lapidary in style, majestic in theme, rich in incident, vivid in characterization – and, sadly but typically, never completed.

Ars longa, vita brevis, as Hippocrates used to say. Tolkien perfected his Method only after decades of work, and had all too short a time to use it before old age and illness robbed him of the power. It was a good method, often a brilliant one, and produced some of the best fantasy fiction ever written. I think it is well worthy of study, more than I have given it here; and I hope that others will use it in ways that Tolkien never could. We have the enormous advantage of not having to invent it for ourselves, and owe the old master a debt that can only be repaid in one way – in new stories, as all literary debts are paid.

THE RHETORIC OF MIDDLE-EARTH

> Do not laugh! But once upon a time (my crest has long since
> fallen) I had a mind to make a body of more or less connected
> legend, ranging from the large and cosmogonic, to the level of
> romantic fairy-story – the larger founded on the lesser in con-
> tact with the earth, the lesser drawing splendour from the vast
> backcloths – which I could dedicate simply to: to England; to
> my country.
> —*The Letters of J. R. R. Tolkien*, no. 131 (to Milton Waldman)

The business of finding and resolving cruxes, of course, is not
the only trick in the philologist's bag, or the only one that Tolkien brought to his imaginative writing. A philologist, in the
nature of things, must have a keen nose for *style,* for the sounds and
usages of words. A genuine document is always rooted in the dialect of
a particular time and place, modified by the author's choice of words,
rhythms, and turns of phrase. Many a forgery has been exposed because of anachronistic language.

Since textual criticism is a branch of philology, it is only natural that
it should suffer when practised by people with no philological skill. Unfortunately, since the eclipse of philology as an academic discipline, most
English-speaking critics have been ignorant of philology and, on the

whole, rather disdainful of the idea that it has anything to teach them. This does not always stop them from making the most sweeping assertions about a text, often on purely ideological grounds. Such critics are fair targets for C. S. Lewis's accusation:

> These men ask me to believe they can read between the lines of the old texts; the evidence is their obvious inability to read (in any sense worth discussing) the lines themselves. They claim to see fern-seed and can't see an elephant ten yards away in broad daylight.

As these critics lose the ability to understand a text, they focus all the harder on the minute details of the text, and lose the benefit of context. This seems paradoxical, but it is, alas, not hard to explain. The 'New Criticism' was invented by men who had not the cultural literacy to see why literature is not and cannot be a science. In the interest of scientific objectivity, they banished the author's intentions and the reader's reactions from their purview. But literature is inherently a subjective art: it is an act of communication between a writer and a reader, and if you leave either of them out of account, the whole art form becomes strictly meaningless.

To rescue criticism from this dead end, the critics imagine they can appeal to 'objective' criteria derived from ideology or psychology instead of the subjective facts of their experience as readers. Hence the elaborate vocabularies of symbolism propounded by various schools: Marxist, feminist, Freudian, Jungian, *etc. ad infinitum*. Whichever code-book is used, the technique is the same. By a process absurdly known as 'close reading', you break the text down into individual words and sentences – syntactic units, not narrative units. On this level you can analyse it without contaminating your objectivity by an emotional reaction. You then look for bits that are 'explained' by your code-book as symbols of something else, and accuse the author of deliberately inserting those symbols with a full (and usually culpable) knowledge of the coded meanings your school of critics has decided to give them. This process is generally known as 'deconstruction'.

In reality, most books are neither written nor read in any such way. What happens, at least with fiction and narrative poetry, occurs on a level *above* the text, to which 'close reading' by its nature gives no access. When I say *above,* I do not mean that this level is superior to the text considered merely as a string of sentences. I mean that this level of narrative is *built* on the text as a house is built on its foundation; it depends on it, is supported by it, and could not stand without it. The foundation is not built for its own sake, but for the purpose of holding up the house. The text does not exist for its own sake; it exists to convey a story.

When you read a story – I speak here of normal recreational readers, not of critics or even editors – you enter a mild trance state. This trance has several interesting properties. It resembles a vivid daydream, but because its materials are furnished or suggested by the author, you as a reader are relieved of the task of making up the events of the daydream and can devote greater attention to imagining its sensuous details. Also, the critical faculties that might impede this imaginative play are partly engaged, and in a way lulled, by the task of reading the words on the page (or, in the case of *told* stories, listening to the narrator's speech). The resulting mental state is mildly psychedelic; it bears some resemblances to the effects of mescaline. Interest in the external environment is diminished; interest in time almost disappears. But where Aldous Huxley on mescaline could spend hours contemplating the folds of his trousers, when you read a story, you contemplate a parallel world, constructed by the author's words out of the materials in your head. Your attention is not on the book, but on the movie playing in your mind: not a flat thing on a screen, but a rounded environment into which you project yourself, either as an observer, or vicariously in the person of one of the characters. Within this environment, your reasoning faculty is fully engaged, but only in particular ways: you want to make sense out of the events, perceive connections between them; above all, you are consumed with a desire to know *what happens next,* and why. This art, or rather the art of inducing such vicarious dreams, is what Tolkien called 'Faërian drama'.

As Samuel Alexander observed, it is psychologically impossible for human beings to *do* a thing and *analyse* it simultaneously. He gave these separate activities the rather unhelpful names of 'Enjoyment' and 'Contemplation'. For my own purposes I prefer the terms *performance* and *attention*. When you look through a telescope, you are attending to the stars and performing astronomy. If you then look *at* the telescope to see how it works, you are attending to the telescope and performing the science of optics. The moment your attention is captured by the instrument instead of the object, your performance moves along with it. This is a general rule; it applies to any activity that requires mental focus.

When you read for enjoyment, you are attending to the story and performing the text – performing it much as an actor performs his lines: bringing it to life in motion and detail, even if you do not read aloud as an actor does. When you read as a critic, or at any rate as a New Critic, you are attending to the text itself and performing the act of textual analysis. This can be a valuable activity. The trouble is that you cannot *attend* to the text while *performing* the text; that is because you cannot focus on the text and the Faërian drama simultaneously. Critics, especially those taught 'close reading' too young, tend to denigrate the whole idea of story; some lose the knack of immersive reading altogether. For such unfortunates, whenever faced with words on a page, their only reaction is sentence-level criticism. The vicarious experience of the story is lost to them for ever.

As a dubious compensation, these critics have the run of academia and the 'literary' reviews. There they can play the game of what B. R. Myers famously called the sentence cult, combing through a text without ever *performing* it, looking for individual sentences that leap to the eye. A bizarre metaphor, a strange cadence, a peculiar word choice, an imitation koan: these are the jewels that the sentence critic gathers. A book like *Ulysses* is perfect for this purpose: Joyce spends so much time doing stylistic jumping-jacks that the *story* is virtually concealed. For us ordinary writers, this would be a terrible mistake. A few *literati* love puzzling out texts, just as some people love crosswords; but the average recreational reader, and especially the kind who devours a novel a week, wants stories.

Our grave danger as writers, then, is that we will do something to wrench the reader's attention away from the story and back to the text. That an insult that he may not lightly forgive. Remember, the reader in the trance is vitally interested in the sequence of time and logic *within* the story: he wants to know what happens next. When we put stumbling-blocks in the text, we yank him away from the fulfilment of that desire and make him focus on an unwanted and (to him) irrelevant problem. This is what is meant by the expression 'bouncing one out of the story'. Readers are reasonably forgiving as a rule, but every bounce will persuade a few to lay the book aside and not return. If we want them to stay with us for the whole journey, we need to keep their minds on the story as much as possible, which generally means keeping it *off* the text.

There are, generally speaking, two ways to do this. The first is to play it safe. If we write plain, flat, unadorned prose, we will never reach for any high emotional or lyrical effects, but then, we will never stumble when we fail. The danger of this style is that it may be too flat to engage the emotions. The second way is more difficult but also more rewarding. That is to write with a broad emotional range, with high points and low points, lyrical passages and plain ones, so that our prose will infect the reader with some of the emotions we wish to induce, and we will not have to depend on the raw impact of the things described. In this, prose style plays a role like the incidental music in a film. It heightens the mood; it enables emotional responses that would seem ridiculous without it.

The first technique is the usual method of melodrama; the second, of drama. It is difficult to predict how readers will respond to a *subtle* event; they may not notice it at all, or it may mean something to them that we did not intend. Melodrama is not subtle; it deals with obvious heroes, obvious villains, obvious problems with clear-cut solutions. A flat prose style can deal with such things, but when it deals with the subtler shades of drama, it either exaggerates them or makes no mark at all. In the first case, the reader is bounced out of the story; in the second, merely bored and confused. You cannot create the Mona Lisa with a sheet of construction paper and a box of crayons.

This, by the way, is the answer to the plaintive question from so many critics (and envious writers), 'Why do X's books sell so well? He can't write his way out of a paper bag.' Dan Brown's prose style is as flat and unaffecting as cardboard; it is, if you like, a 'bad' style. But it is appropriate for melodrama; and the elements of melodrama exist on the level of story, not text. It has been said that a melodrama is a story about a Villain, a Victim, and a Rescuer. These roles are all defined by the characters' actions, not by anything you will find through sentence-level analysis. When George Orwell talked about 'good bad books', he meant just the kind of book that tells a melodramatic story in a limited prose style, but tells it vividly and is therefore entertaining and effective.

Many critics have claimed that Tolkien is a bad prose stylist. Does this mean that *The Lord of the Rings* is a 'good bad book', merely an entertaining melodrama? To answer the question, we need to define the difference between melodrama and drama. I am indebted to Stephen R. Donaldson for this partial but useful definition: Where melodrama is about a Villain, a Victim, and a Rescuer, drama is about how those three characters exchange roles.

Gollum is an excellent example. When we meet him in *The Two Towers,* he appears to be a pure villain, with Frodo and Sam as his intended victims. But Frodo tames him, for a while, just enough so that Gollum can play the rescuer in the Dead Marshes. Captured by Faramir, he becomes a victim, and Frodo rescues him. He is victimized in another way by Sam, who fails to see how Gollum is struggling towards the good, and inadvertently pushes him back into his evil habits. Then Gollum becomes the villain once more, betraying the Hobbits to Shelob; but in the end, at Mount Doom itself, he turns (despite his worst intentions) into the final rescuer who saves the Quest from catastrophe.

Whatever *The Lord of the Rings* is, it is not a melodrama, any more than *Hamlet* or the *Iliad.* It contains several dramas, interlaced in a complex pattern, and each told in a style appropriate to the incidents and the characters. But none of these styles are the default style of the modern 'literary' novel. There are no showpiece sentences for the critics to make much of; there is no stock vocabulary of symbolism, Freudian, Marxist, or what not, by which to decode the text.

Indeed the text of *The Lord of the Rings* is very different from that of the modern novel, because it says what it means, and means (at minimum) what it says. This, too, is a necessary feature of fantasy. The Ring is not a symbolic reification of Frodo's will to power, but a real physical object – real in the context of the story – which happens to actually *confer* power. Critics are apt to confuse the two. One could deliberately choose to read the Ring symbolically; but then, one could 'read' an actual motorcar as a 'symbol' of the desire to travel rapidly. Dark Lords in Middle-earth have Rings of Power, and people in that equally wild fantasy world, the Industrialized West, drive cars. As Tolkien himself said: 'The story is really a story of what happened in B.C. year X, and it just happened to people who were like that!' As such, it resists all attempts to analyse it by Modernist or Postmodernist methods. You cannot take the text simply as a text; to find out what it means, you have to experience it as a story.

A more promising line of attack blames Tolkien for not writing in the usual language of the English literary novel *circa* 1950. His style is usually criticized on two different grounds, or three. The opening chapters of *The Fellowship of the Ring* are denounced for their slightly old-fashioned tone, reminiscent (it is said) of Victorian penny dreadfuls and Edwardian school stories. The other two volumes repel many critics (and some readers) because of their archaic language. The third criticism is that Tolkien has no consistent style, but veers all over the place. In fact this variation of style was done deliberately and expertly, and the story could not be effectually told without it.

One of the most common bits of advice offered to young writers is to 'find your own voice' and then stick with it. This is some of the worst advice a writer can take. Ernest Hemingway took it, wrote three or four strikingly original books, and then spent the rest of his life writing pastiches of his earlier style. Tolkien never fell into that trap. He knew that each story demands its own voice. A fairy-story like *The Hobbit* should not be told in the same tone as a creation myth like the *Ainulindalë,* or a tragedy like *The Children of Húrin,* or a light farce like *Farmer Giles of Ham.* In *The Lord of the Rings* we see the whole regiment of Tolkien's styles on parade, beginning with the lightest and most quotidian, climbing by degrees to the highest and most formal.

The story begins in a jolly Edwardian style that at least one hostile reviewer compared to the *Boys Own Paper.* This very mild dose of archaism does two necessary things. First, it distances the narrative from the purely modern novel: this cleanses the palate, and prepares the reader for something fresh. Second, it *places* the story culturally, by alluding to the nearest familiar equivalent. Tolkien once described the Shire as 'more or less a Warwickshire village of about the period of the Diamond Jubilee'. The various Hobbit-dialects, from the rustic talk of Gaffer Gamgee to the lighthearted blather of Merry and Pippin, faithfully recreate modes of diction from that place and time.

The last twenty years before the First World War were a time of peace and unexampled prosperity in England. Through all the popular novels, plays, and songs of the period there runs a kind of fat-bellied optimism, a refusal to be impressed by anything old or foreign, and especially by anything unpleasant. Such things could always be dismissed by the magic formula, 'It can't happen *here.*' With the coming of war, the spell stopped working, the bubble burst, and English speech and thought necessarily changed. As George Orwell pointed out, the pre-war style is preserved in the stories of P. G. Wodehouse:

> Conceived in 1917 or thereabouts, Bertie [Wooster] really belongs to an epoch earlier than that.... 'He was still living in the period about which he wrote,' says Flannery, meaning, probably, the nineteen-twenties. But the period was really the Edwardian age, and Bertie Wooster, if he ever existed, was killed round about 1915.

If there had been a real Bertie Wooster, a wealthy young Edwardian man-about-town, he might not have been physically killed in 1915; but he would have been a changed man after Passchendaele and the Somme. The lighthearted assumption that progress was inevitable, and that only the comfortable life was real, would have been blown out of him by the mighty blasts of the German artillery.

Now, this is precisely the assumption that the Hobbits have at the out-set of *The Lord of the Rings*. The 'Days of Dearth' are long past; the Shire is protected, secretly and unobtrusively, by the Rangers, just as England was protected by the Royal Navy. The average Edwardian Englishman thought foreigners were too silly and comical for words; Hobbits did not even bother to show the outside world on their maps. An English squire of 1910 talked like a Hobbit squire of Bilbo's time; an Englishman of 1940 (when squires, in the old sense, hardly existed any longer) could hardly have been mistaken for either of them.

But this Edwardian style is only the first course in a rich and varied banquet. As soon as the Hobbits leave the Shire, the style begins to break down in an artfully arranged manner. The description of the Old Forest is severe and estranging. The narrative becomes more sober in tone, the Hobbit-talk forced and unconvincing, until even the Hobbits' attempts at song are crushed out by the sinister atmosphere of Old Man Willow. Some passages of description at this point are written in a style curiously reminiscent of the 'stage-directions' in parts of *Ulysses*. In the chapters from 'The Old Forest' to 'Fog on the Barrow-downs', the effect is one of sustained phantasmagoria.

In this setting, and almost of a piece with it, is the voice of Tom Bom-badil, who speaks in verse – a slightly looser version of the rough metre of his signature song. The four Hobbits have been rescued from an estrang-ing environment, but their rescuer is stranger than the Old Forest itself. It does not do Bombadil much injustice to call him *inconsequent*: evil has no power over him, either to change him or to constrain him, but nei-ther has he any power over it except for small personal interventions. His song (*Ring a dong dillo!*) is a string of nonsense, a spell against the grim and perilous *sense* of the Willow and the Barrow-wights. He can deliver the Hobbits from the consequences of their mistakes, but he lacks the power to bring about any consequences of his own. In today's parlance, Bombadil is *trippy*. When Beard and Kenney, in *Bored of the Rings,* made 'Tim Benzedrine' a drug-addled, draft-dodging hippie, they rose from mere parody to trenchant criticism.

Next the Hobbits arrive in Bree. Like the Shire, Bree is inhabited (but only partly) by Hobbits, and protected (but only partly) by the Rangers. Both are what Clute & Grant, in the *Encyclopaedia of Fantasy,* call 'polders'; but the dykes surrounding Bree are thinner, and cannot keep out the Black Riders even for a single night. The style of the Bree chapters is a partial return to the Edwardian style, but a deliberately unsuccessful one. The comfortable Hobbit-life of the Bree-land has been diminished by 'thinning', to take another term from Clute & Grant; and the text is correspondingly 'thinned' as well. Frodo ventures a comic song, his first since leaving the Shire; but such levity is dangerous here, and nearly proves fatal. And Gandalf has failed to appear. The Quest seems lost before it has fairly begun; Hobbitry cannot face the Wild alone, any more than one could be a comfortable Edwardian gentleman without the protection of the British Empire.

It is here that we see the first important appearance of the style that will predominate in the later 'books' of the tale. We might call it Tolkien's *neo-archaic* style: it is archaic in tone and diction, but he carefully refrains (at this point) from using archaic words. Aragorn is the first major character to employ it in dialogue. He is a personage out of an older and nobler world: the leader, in fact, of the unseen protectors who have hitherto preserved the Shire. Once he enters the story, the narrative tone becomes more formal, the prose more cadenced. It is not yet archaic in the strict sense: the words are all familiar to us, except for proper names and a few words of Shire-dialect. But the sentence structure begins to approximate an older diction. It is beginning to be the language of the sagas, dignified, musical, and evocative.

Such language is routinely deplored by modern-minded people, who suffer from what Owen Barfield called 'chronological snobbery'. In fact, this degree of archaism is still used for effect by quite ordinary writers;

even by politicians. John F. Kennedy's inaugural address used the trick to good effect: 'Ask not what your country can do for you.' Change *Ask not* to *Don't ask,* and the sentence loses force and rhythm. Change it to *Do not ask,* and the effect is even worse: it turns from an inspirational speech into a priggish prohibition. Most of the archaism in *The Lord of the Rings* is on this level, and Tolkien uses it judiciously and well.

As the road to Rivendell grows more perilous, and the Black Riders hotter on Frodo's trail, the narrative style becomes still more serious and uncompromising. At times the descriptions of scenes and action recall the unadorned vigour and economy of military reportage: the language of Caesar's *Commentaries* or U. S. Grant's memoirs. This reportage is leavened with just enough interior description to remind us of Frodo's growing weakness and emotional struggle. Even the visible help of Glorfindel, and the unseen aid of Elrond and Gandalf, barely bring him to his destination alive; and Book I ends with Frodo unconscious, not knowing whether he has been rescued by the Elves, or captured by the Ringwraiths, or swept away by the flooding river.

The second movement of a symphony typically opens with a theme recognizably related to the first movement, but slower and more subdued, often in a minor key. The opening of Book II is, by that standard, musically perfect. Bilbo reappears; Gandalf reappears – but Bilbo has aged, and Gandalf is consumed by urgent cares. The whole tone is more serious, and despite occasional patches of Hobbit-talk, the Edwardian style is more or less gone for good. But before Tolkien settles down to the neo-archaic style, he presents us with a smorgasbord at the Council of Elrond.

Aristotle, in his *Poetics,* remarks that a poet can represent men either as better than life, worse than life, or just as they are. Northrop Frye has labelled those modes *romantic, ironic,* and *mimetic,* respectively. He then divides the mimetic mode into 'high mimetic', which deals with strong and heroic characters in a realistic way, and 'low mimetic', which deals largely with the characters and incidents of everyday life. To this he adds, at the top of the scale, the *mythic* mode, which deals with gods and other supernatural beings. Hobbit-talk is low mimetic; Aragorn is high mimetic at first, gradually ascending to the romantic as he grows from 'Strider' into 'King Elessar'. The Council of Elrond is described in a mimetic style, 'high' in subject-matter and tone, but 'low' in that it realistically depicts the bickerings, misunderstandings, and confused agendas of a badly-run meeting. As Tom Shippey points out, Elrond may be a legendary hero, but he is not much of a chairman. However, these chaotic proceedings give full play to four of Frye's five modes – all but the mythic – and some of Tolkien's subtlest writing.

Each speaker has a distinct style, suited to his circumstances and to the story he tells. Gimli does a stellar turn in an old formal style, describing the visit of Sauron's menacing ambassador to King Dáin. Boromir operates in the romantic mode, in the realm of prophetic dreams and ancient legends, and is answered by Aragorn in the same mode. Legolas gives high-mimetic reportage of Gollum's detention and escape. The most interesting speaker is Gandalf, and his best turn comes in describing the treason of Saruman – who has the one really modern voice in the book. Saruman's speeches are naked propaganda, as dishonest as Goebbels' broadcasts or the leading articles in *Pravda*. Later, hearing him first-hand, Gimli will exclaim indignantly: 'The words of this wizard stand on their heads.' That could as easily describe George Orwell's 'Newspeak'.

The Council of Elrond shows one of the great advantages of Tolkien's strategic use of style. Each character's dialogue remains more or less on the level of the narrative at the point where he entered the story. In this way, nobody's speech patterns (except Gollum's) ever seem incongruous when they first appear; and because we grow used to them, they do not seem incongruous even when the style of the narrative changes and they remain the same. The Hobbits continue their light and informal Edwardian talk; Aragorn continues to talk like a sober man of honour, not only born but tried by fire to be a leader. Gandalf never quite loses the slightly humorous waspishness he first showed in *The Hobbit*, as when he snaps at Pippin in Moria:

'Fool of a Took!' he growled. 'This is a serious journey, not a hobbit walking-party. Throw yourself in next time, and then you will be no further nuisance.'

In 'The Breaking of the Fellowship', we see another brief touch of phantasmagoria when Frodo looks across Middle-earth from Amon Hen, and nearly gives himself away to Sauron. Once again this serves as a kind of caesura, emphatically separating a comparatively safe and comfortable part of the story from the sharply increased perils and higher tone that come after; but, of course, on a higher level than before. This time it is Gandalf's voice (never identified by name) that calls Frodo back from the brink of disaster: 'Fool, take it off! Take off the Ring!' This interlude sets up the dire situation in *The Two Towers*: Boromir is slain, the Quest divided; Merry and Pippin are captured, Frodo and Sam are alone on the way to Mordor.

Tolkien himself observed, many years later, that *The Fellowship of the Ring* was very different in tone from the other two volumes. From the beginning of *The Two Towers*, the narrative achieves an approximately level and consistent tone, which I have referred to as the neo-archaic style. Book IV, concerned with the doings of Frodo and Sam, relaxes slightly towards the level of the Hobbits' dialogue; the Rohan chapters stiffen into definite and formal archaism. Hugh Brogan roundly criticized this archaism when it occurred in the chapter 'The King of the Golden Hall', and called it 'tushery'. This term, as Tolkien said in his reply, properly refers to the use of expletives to produce a false archaic effect: *tush, zounds, marry,* and so forth. He denied (with justified indignation) that he had done anything of the kind. He gave an example of 'watered archaism' (as he calls it) from *The Two Towers*, along with a modern English paraphrase. The speaker here is Théoden:

> 'Nay, Gandalf!' said the King. 'You do not know your own skill in healing. It shall not be so. I myself will go to war, to fall in the front of the battle, if it must be. Thus shall I sleep better.'

Here is the modernized version:

> 'Not at all my dear G. You don't know your own skill as a doc-
> tor. Things aren't going to be like that. I shall go to the war in
> person, even if I have to be one of the first casualties.'

'And then what?' Tolkien asks. People who talk like that do not say things like 'Thus shall I sleep better' when talking about death. Indeed, modern people have a horror of talking about death at all. It would be, as he calls it, 'an insincerity of thought, a disunion of word and meaning'. People who talk in modern dialects do not bother about how they will rest in their graves. Either they have modern religious beliefs, and think they will be in Heaven (or Hell) with other things to think about, or they have no religion at all, and no belief in an afterlife. Even the modern, California-style Western Buddhists hardly count as an exception: to the extent that they talk about the afterlife in Buddhist terms, they are using imported terminology, and so not using modern English idioms at all.

The Riders of Rohan are the purest representation (and idealization) of 'Northernness' in *The Lord of the Rings*. Theirs is a 'virtuous pagan' culture, sanitized by comparison with any actual pagan society; but sanitized in the same way as the Danes and Geats in *Beowulf*. The good qualities of the pagan Teuton, the fine sense of honour, the tremendous personal courage even in the face of certain defeat, are emphasized; the faults are largely glossed over in silence. Rohan has many songs but few books, just as ancient Germanic society (despite the occasional use of runic inscriptions) was essentially pre-literate. In such a society, personal honour takes the place of written documents; poetry and high speech take the place of literature. *Beowulf* and the sagas are the perfect expressions of this culture in narrative form. It should be no surprise that Tolkien approaches closest to their diction when he portrays a similar culture.

One more style appears in dialogue in *The Two Towers:* the diction of the Orcs. This is almost as modern a style as Saruman's, though not quite, because this kind of degraded speech, though more common now than formerly, has been current in 'low' English society for centuries. Unlike the cod Cockney of the trolls in *The Hobbit* (which Tolkien soon came to regret), it is not primarily distinguished by class-markers. Tolkien took pains to point out to the dramatizers at the BBC that Orcs did not drop their aitches. What this style does, with a skill necessary in those days and almost forgotten now, is to suggest a squalid and vulgar mode of speech without actually spattering the page with obscenities. When Uglúk and Grishnákh use words like 'filth', or the Orc slave-driver in Mordor says 'I reckon eyes are better than your snotty noses', the reader is meant to infer that these are merely cleaned-up renditions of what they actually said. Tolkien explains in the Appendices:

> Orcs and Trolls spoke as they would, without love of words or things; and their language was actually more degraded and filthy than I have shown it. . . . Much the same sort of talk can still be heard among the orc-minded; dreary and repetitive with hatred and contempt, too long removed from good to retain even verbal vigour, save in the ears of those to whom only the squalid sounds strong.

'Orc-mindedness', alas, is treated as an actual virtue by some modern critics, who call it 'authenticity' and suppose that only a prude could object. But in fact the squalid does not sound strong; and some readers are beginning to oppose it out of sheer boredom. How Tolkien represented Orc-talk without obscenities, yet also without the twee euphemisms then common in printed English, is a technique deserving of study.

I have mentioned how each major character tends to stick closely to the style and diction that prevailed in the book at the time when he first appeared. This provides one of the richest elements in Tolkien's stylistic tapestry: the juxtaposition of widely different speaking styles, sometimes moving, sometimes comical. Occasionally the joke arises from the lower character's incomprehension, as when the Hobbits return to the Shire wearing armour, and Gaffer Gamgee asks about Sam: 'What's come of his weskit? I don't hold with wearing ironmongery, whether it wears well or no.' In general, though, he does not mock the higher speaker for pretension, or the lower for vulgarity. We laugh simply because two characters are finding such different ways of saying the same thing, and are glad because they understand each other. So it is when Théoden meets Merry and Pippin:

> 'Farewell, my hobbits! May we meet again in my house! There you shall sit beside me and tell me all that your hearts desire: the deeds of your grandsires, as far back as you can reckon them; and we will speak also of Tobold the Old and his herblore. Farewell!'
>
> 'So that is the King of Rohan,' said Pippin in an undertone. 'A fine old fellow. Very polite.'

Perhaps the finest moment of this kind comes when Faramir and Sam exchange courtesies, each in his own peculiar idiom:

> Sam hesitated for a moment, then bowing very low: 'Good night, Captain, my lord,' he said. 'You took the chance, sir.'
>
> 'Did I so?' said Faramir.
>
> 'Yes sir, and showed your quality: the very highest.'
>
> Faramir smiled. 'A pert servant, Master Samwise. But nay: the praise of the praiseworthy is above all rewards.'

In Middle-earth, only one thing is better than the praise of the praiseworthy. That is the praise due to those who have vowed the impossible and kept their vows; and to that, accordingly, I shall turn next.

FRODO'S VAUNT

'Faithless is he that says farewell when the road darkens,'
said Gimli.

'Maybe,' said Elrond, 'but let him not vow to walk in the
dark, who has not seen the nightfall.'

'Yet sworn word may strengthen quaking heart,' said Gimli.

'Or break it,' said Elrond.

—*The Lord of the Rings,* Book II, chapter 3

I t occasionally happened in mediaeval Europe that a man, especially a knight or noble, would make an extravagant and boasting
promise, apparently out of sheer unmotivated bravado, and then
risk his life to fulfil it – or lose it rather than fail. Such promises were
often called *vaunts:* not an unmixed compliment, for the word is related
to *vanity.* But the heroic vaunt became a fixture in mediaeval literature,
where it was glamorized and taken up into the standard equipment of
the hero. The mediaeval hero was supposed to be a man of infinite honour, who, having once pledged his word to any cause, would die rather
than see it fail. We find a similar quality in ancient Sparta, where a man
was shamed beyond redemption unless he returned from battle 'with

his shield or on it'. But the mediaeval vaunt was individual and voluntary, where the Spartan military code was the same for every citizen.

The ancient Germanic peoples, to judge by their poetry (and their curious manner of making war), were much addicted to this practice of making outrageous boasts – often in their cups before a battle – and then risking everything, not only life but victory, in reckless deeds to achieve what they had recklessly sworn. In a preliterate society, without banks or credit agencies, criminal records or background checks, a man's word had to be his bond: and the more difficult the things he vowed to do, the higher his standing would be if he achieved them. This attitude existed (and exists) among many peoples besides the Germans; the very history of the word *credit* shows it. In Latin it was *creditum*, 'that which is believed'; it was the measure of a man's willingness to fulfil his obligations as much as his capacity to pay his debts.

Useful as it was in societies without sophisticated record-keeping, this kind of credit was not an unmixed virtue. In his essay 'Ofermod', Tolkien observes:

> For this 'northern heroic spirit' is never quite pure; it is of gold and an alloy. Unalloyed it would direct a man to endure even death unflinching, when necessary: that is when death may help the achievement of some object of will, or when life can only be purchased by denial of what one stands for. But since such conduct is held admirable, the alloy of personal good name was never wholly absent.

In early modern times, the spread of literacy and the monetization of wealth reduced the need for such punctilious attention to personal honour; and a certain sluggish and bourgeois smugness, born in part from the sneers of Enlightenment *philosophes,* derided the old codes of honour as anachronisms, and made them objects of ridicule. For a while in the twentieth century, when the world was threatened by the greatest horrors it had yet seen, even smug and 'philosophical' people could appreciate the need for heroes, and for people who *talked* like heroes – people

47

who promised to do great things, and could be trusted to do their utmost to keep those promises. The history of the Second World War and the Cold War are filled with vaunts that were, indeed, at least partially lived up to. Thus Winston Churchill:

> We shall fight on the beaches, we shall fight on the landing grounds, we shall fight in the fields and in the streets, we shall fight in the hills; we shall never surrender. . . .

It is no accident that John F. Kennedy's inaugural speech, with its archaic turns of phrase (such as *Ask not*), contained a vaunt that would have adorned any knight's speech from a mediaeval romance:

> Let every nation know, whether it wishes us well or ill, that we shall pay any price, bear any burden, meet any hardship, support any friend, oppose any foe, in order to assure the survival and the success of liberty.

It is the exact tone of Roland swearing to defend the pass at Roncesvalles. If a mediaeval audience had heard Kennedy speaking this words, it would *demand* their fulfilment, even in the long nightmare of Vietnam; would, indeed, criticize his successors only for fulfilling the vaunt halfheartedly, trying for a stalemate instead of full-blooded victory. *Any friend* included even so unsavoury a character as Nguyen Van Thieu; *any hardship* included sending half a million soldiers halfway round the world, and seeing fifty thousand return in body bags. It may have been unwise in the extreme to make such a promise, as even a mediaeval audience could readily see; but according to the code of the vaunt, Kennedy gained standing (what Malory would call *worship*) by making it, and would lose all honour by breaking it.

Sometimes the vaunt is short and simple, without any high-flown rhetoric, but with the blunt force and plainness characteristic of military men. One of the most famous vaunts of the twentieth century came from Gen. Douglas MacArthur:

I came out of Bataan and I shall return.

A promise which he amply fulfilled. It fits well with Tolkien's observation in 'Ofermod' that MacArthur's superiors asked him to modify his promise to *We shall return,* and he refused. For him, it was not only a matter of policy, but of personal honour. In the end, like Beowulf fighting the dragon single-handed, he took on a foe beyond his measure and led his command to disaster in the Yalu campaign of the Korean War; his military career ended in the ignominy of a vaunt unfulfilled.

A frequent feature of literary vaunts is that the hero not only promises to achieve a superhuman task, he places needless restrictions on himself; he fights, as it were, with one hand voluntarily tied behind his back, because that more clearly shows off his superiority. Such things, as the mediaeval poets well knew, often led to disaster. One of Tolkien's most important scholarly works was his commentary on *The Battle of Maldon.* The English leader, Beorhtnoth, not only promises to defeat the invading Danes, he offers to make it an even contest by letting them disembark from their ships and form up for battle on dry land:

> Ða se eorl ongan for his ofermode
> alyfan landes to fela laþere ðeode.

So wrote the poet; and it used to be translated 'Then the earl in his over-boldness gave too much ground to the hated people'. Tolkien pointed out that the phrase *to fela,* in Old English texts, is always used with a strong tone of condemnation. On his reading, the phrase should be translated, 'Then the earl in his overweening pride gave ground to the enemy, as he should not have done'. The result, predictably, was the loss of the war. Beorhtnoth lost his life and threw away his army in a foolhardy attempt to make the victory over the Danes 'sporting' and therefore more glamorous. Beowulf (said Tolkien) commits the exact same error as Beorhtnoth, and with as little excuse:

Yet he does not rid himself of his chivalry, the excess persists, even when he is an old king upon whom all the hopes of a people rest. He will not deign to lead a force against the dragon, as wisdom might direct even a hero to do; for, as he explains in a long 'vaunt', his many victories have relieved him of fear. . . . He is saved from defeat, and the essential object, destruction of the dragon, only achieved by the loyalty of a subordinate. Beowulf's chivalry would otherwise have ended in his own useless death, with the dragon still at large.

A few characters in *The Lord of the Rings* operate on this moral level. Denethor and Boromir make no vaunts that we hear of on stage, as it were; but both of them fight and die in the manner of men who cannot bear to survive the downfall of their honour. However, *The Lord of the Rings* is not really a tale about pagans or mediaeval Christians; it is a tale chiefly about virtuous and idealized pre-Christians, *animae naturaliter Christianae,* who have preserved a vague knowledge of the one God (such as Melchizedek had, according to the Bible) and at least have resisted all the blandishments of foul cults and idol-worship.

Indeed Melchizedek, who was a king as well as a monotheistic priest, may have served as a model for the priest-kings of Númenor; just as the ancient Semitic languages influenced the Adûnaic language that Tolkien invented for that country. When the kings of Númenor broke their friendship with the Elves, they began to take Adûnaic names: Ar-Adûnakhôr, Ar-Zimrathôn, and so on, down to Ar-Pharazôn the Golden. Purely in terms of sound, *Ar-Melchizedek* would make a perfectly plausible Adûnaic king-name.

As we might expect, these virtuous pagans, these pre-Abrahamic monotheists, have their own equally idealized and purified version of the vaunt. Nearly the whole plot of *The Lord of the Rings* is adumbrated in the form of vaunts by various characters, which take the place that in fantasy is often held by prophecy. It is part of the 'fey' tradition that Tolkien brings with him from *The Silmarillion* (and thence from his sources), where a character's dying utterances, or speeches made in other moments of white-hot passion and clarity, have special meaning and significance: as with the dying words of Fëanor, or some of the rash pronouncements that Túrin made and would live to regret. In what we might call the providential economy of Middle-earth, the vaunt is a glimpse of the future; what Aristotle would call a final cause – a goal that will shape and determine the actions of the speaker from that moment forward.

The vaunts begin exactly when the book begins to use what I have called the neo-archaic style: with the arrival of Aragorn at *The Prancing Pony*. His first vaunt is still in the voice of 'Strider' rather than 'Aragorn' or 'King Elessar', but it strikes a note of *gravitas* that we have not previously heard from any of the characters; not even, quite, from Gandalf. In the very same sentence where he first acknowledges his true name to Frodo, he pledges himself to an unlimited liability:

> 'I am Aragorn son of Arathorn; and if by life or death I can save you, I will.'

No time limit is stated; no conceivable danger is excluded. Aragorn has given Frodo a blank cheque for whatever help he needs, wherever and whenever he needs it. Later, indeed, Aragorn's efforts to save Frodo and the Quest by diverting Sauron's attention will dictate the whole course of the war in Gondor.

Later, when that war has reached a critical stage, Aragorn makes another vaunt, to Éomer this time, whose fulfilment changes the whole strategic map and creates the victory of the Pelennor Fields. He is about to lead Legolas and Gimli (and the Rangers) into the Paths of the Dead, and Éomer fears he is throwing away all these lives for nothing:

> 'Alas! Aragorn my friend!' said Éomer. 'I had hoped that we should ride to war together; but if you seek the Paths of the Dead, then our parting is come, and it is little likely that we shall ever meet again under the Sun.'

> 'That road I will take, nonetheless,' said Aragorn. 'But I say
> to you, Éomer, that in battle we may yet meet again, though all
> the hosts of Mordor should stand between.'

So indeed it falls out, when Aragorn brings the black fleet up the Anduin to help the newly arrived Rohirrim break the siege of Minas Tirith; and he duly reminds Éomer of his vaunt. It is, perhaps, the closest any non-Hobbit character comes to saying 'I told you so'.

The Rohirrim, who have just the kind of preliterate culture in which personal honour and the vaunt mean most – 'heroic' in the anthropological sense – naturally have developed vaunting into a high art form. Théoden's speech to Gandalf, previously discussed, contains as good a vaunt as anyone could make: 'I myself will go to war, to fall in the front of the battle, if it must be.' This promise he keeps to the letter, and though he dies, his death purchases an indispensable victory.

The role of honour as credit is manifest in Rohan on every level. Háma admits Gandalf and company to King Théoden's hall because he is a good judge of character, and considers them worthy of such trust. Sauron steals horses from the Rohirrim, but despite great pressure they refuse to buy safety by paying a tribute of horses. Boromir rightly dismisses that rumour with scorn: 'They love their horses next to their kin.'

The realm of Rohan itself is founded upon a bond of honour; for Eorl the Young promised undying alliance with Gondor in exchange for the land that the Stewards gave him. At the time of the War of the Ring, the alliance has already lasted five hundred years: longer than almost any alliance recorded in the real world, but not an impossible length of time. England and Portugal are allies to this day under a treaty signed in 1386; but even that alliance was regrettably interrupted for a time, when Portugal came under the rule of the Spanish crown.

In Middle-earth, where the vaunt is both prophecy and destiny, Eorl's words have the power to bind his whole nation without any such tergiversations. No Rider of Rohan would so much as think of going back on this national commitment to the Men of Gondor, though it was made centuries before he was born. This is one of many points that Peter Jackson's films not only ignore but positively contradict: the Théoden of the films has to be coaxed and coerced into aiding Gondor. Jackson does not understand the vaunt; this whole layer of meaning in the story is absent from his version. The only man of Rohan in the *book* who could have behaved so basely is Wormtongue.

On a slightly lower rhetorical level, we have Treebeard's resolution to deal with Saruman, even if it means the last march of the Ents; and Merry and Pippin's vow to stick with Frodo through thick and thin, which leads them to follow him on the road to Mordor, and eventually to their separate heroic roles in the War of the Ring. And of course there is Sam's promise, made after he jumps into the Anduin without knowing how to swim, in his desperation to prevent Frodo from having to face Mordor alone:

> 'It would be the death of you to come with me, Sam,' said
> Frodo, 'and I could not have borne that.'
> 'Not as certain as being left behind,' said Sam.
> 'But I am going to Mordor.'
> 'I know that well enough, Mr. Frodo. Of course you are.
> And I'm coming with you.'

Like so many things in Middle-earth (and in real life), the vaunt has an evil shadow or parody – the threat. Sauron's messengers are capable of couching threats in the most elegant rhetoric, at once menacing and diplomatic. They use both the carrot and the stick, and the promises of the 'carrot' are as extravagant as the vaunts of the heroes. When Sauron sends his ambassador to King Dáin at Erebor, the language recalls the idiom of the Norse sagas (on which the cultures of Dale and the Mountain are largely based). Here the vaunt takes a grim political form:

> '. . . It is but a trifle that Sauron fancies, and an earnest of your
> good will. Find it, and three rings that the Dwarf-sires pos-
> sessed of old shall be returned to you, and the realm of Moria
> shall be yours for ever. Find only news of the thief, whether he
> still lives and where, and you shall have great reward and last-

ing friendship from the Lord. Refuse, and things will not seem
so well. Do you refuse?'

At that his breath came like the hiss of snakes, and all who
stood by shuddered, but Dáin said: 'I say neither yea nor nay.
I must consider this message and what it means under its fair
cloak.'

'Consider well, but not too long,' said he.

'The time of my thought is my own to spend,' answered
Dáin.

'For the present,' said he, and rode into the darkness.

The price offered is an extravagant one, and a Dwarf-king, of all
people, will be shrewd enough to know what this means: the thing demanded is a harder matter than it seems. The threat at the end, vague and
open-ended but clearly ominous, is more than enough to confirm Dáin's
suspicions; so he sends Glóin off to consult Elrond, and with him his son
Gimli – and thereby hangs a tale.

Still it is characteristic that evil, while it can parody the good, cannot
achieve its ends: *Oft evil will shall evil mar.* Sauron's blandishments fail to
win over the Dwarves of the Mountain. Saruman's spell does not convince either Gandalf or Théoden. When the Mouth of Sauron dictates
terms to Aragorn's apparently defeated army, and makes them sound
magnanimous, Gandalf rejects them with scorn, complete with a dissection of the language to show just how hollow the offered terms really are.
And the Orcs, while they do a good deal of bragging, never connect it
with any kind of action at all. Their bold words are only hot air, which is
an atmosphere poisonous to the vaunt. You cannot even have the fun of
making a vow unless you are in the habit of meaning what you say.

Hobbits, as a rule, are not given to high-flown rhetoric or extravagant
promises; but each of the principal Hobbit characters makes a vaunt, in
characteristically lighthearted and low-key language, and all but one, in
the end, keep their vows. The only exception is Bilbo, moved by the plight
of the West to make an offer beyond his power, which is gently refused by

the Council of Elrond. After all the high-minded and 'romantic' debates (in Northrop Frye's sense of the word), Bilbo tries to take up the burden of the Quest with an 'ironic' version of a vaunt: 'Bilbo the silly hobbit started this affair, and Bilbo had better finish it, or himself.' The words, as Gandalf points out, are lightly spoken but seriously meant. But this is too great a task for Bilbo, weakened by old age and already partly corrupted by long years of keeping the Ring.

So instead Frodo volunteers, in a 'mimetic' vaunt of his own, the most plainspoken of all. It is hard to conceive of a vaunt being made timidly, but Frodo manages it: 'I will take the Ring, though I do not know the way.' He is not making a boast; he is not trying to claim superiority over any of the great and wise people present. He is only offering to bear the burden to the end, until either he or the Ring is destroyed. In the terms of 'Ofermod', he has the gold of the 'northern heroic spirit' *without* the alloy. He will endure even death unflinching, if that is necessary (as it nearly is); and he will do so without regard for his personal good name. When he returns to the Shire, he does not even talk about why he has been away, and Sam is saddened to see how little honour the Ringbearer has in his own country.

If each character's vaunts codify his actions and fill them with purpose, Frodo's vaunt drives the whole story of *The Lord of the Rings*. Indeed, one could say, it was the vaunt that made his success possible; or rather, his vaunt and his success both sprang from his essential humility. Bilbo took so little harm from the Ring, says Gandalf, because he began with pity. Frodo bore the burden to the bitter end because he began with the unalloyed gold – the willingness to do great deeds, unmixed with the desire for fame. He took up the Quest without boasting, without pride, without self-aggrandizement; he went to the cannon's mouth for reasons that had nothing to do with the bubble reputation. His was the hardest vaunt, the least boastful, the most reluctant; and in the end, by steadfast help and the gift of grace, it was achieved.

THE METHOD AND THE MORGOTH

As Tom Shippey observes in *The Road to Middle-earth* and *Author of the Century*, Tolkien worked largely by seizing upon apparent lacunae and contradictions in the legends he loved, and tried to invent 'asterisk-versions' of what he thought the lost material must have been like. He announced his intentions frankly when he called his earliest cycle of myths 'The Book of Lost Tales', and dedicated it to England, or to the English. One of the earliest Tales, 'Turambar and the Foalókë', began with Tolkien's attempt to work out the motifs he found in the tale of Kullervo from the *Kalevala*, married indissolubly with a dragon right out of the *Völsunga saga*. It boggles the mind to think that this very same tale, after nearly a century of transformations, was issued in finished form as *The Children of Húrin*. All these things – the cross-fertilization of mythologies, the development of themes the ancients barely sketched in outline, the painfully slow gestation and long-delayed publication – typify the Tolkien Method almost to the point of self-parody.

The twelve volumes of *The History of Middle-earth* provide an exhaustive course in that Method: no other major writer that I know of has left such a complete record of his working process, or had so obligingly meticulous an editor. *Morgoth's Ring* takes up the story in 1948, when Tolkien was working furiously on *The Return of the King* (a process described in the previous volume of the *History*), and paused to consider the far-reaching effects that *The Lord of the Rings* must have on the earlier legendarium.

The first step was to re-examine the creation myth of the Eldar, now known as the *Ainulindalë*. This was one of the oldest Tales in terms of continuous development, for it went back to the first version of 'The Music of the Ainur', written after the 1914–18 war ended, but before he left the staff of the Oxford English Dictionary in the spring of 1920. Most of the tales in *The Silmarillion* were rewritten from memory after 1925, based on the 'Sketch of the Mythology'. The *Ainulindalë* is among the very few places where one can trace the development of specific details right back to the 'Lost Tales'.

First Tolkien seems to have dug up the *Ainulindalë* as he had left it before beginning work on 'the new Hobbit' in 1937. As he nearly always did when looking at old work, he found it deeply unsatisfactory and virtually began the whole work over again. But this time he did so not just once, but twice in rapid succession. As Christopher Tolkien explains it:

> So drastic was the revision (with a great deal of new material written on the blank verso pages) that in the result two distinct texts of the work, wholly divergent in essential respects, exist physically in the same manuscript. . . .
>
> But there is another text, a typescript made by my father, that was also directly based on *Ainulindalë* B of the 1930s; and in this there appears a much more radical – one might say a devastating – change in the cosmology: for in this version the Sun is already in existence from the beginning of Arda.

It was this 'Copernican revolution' in *The Silmarillion* that dominated and in the end defeated all Tolkien's later work on the legends of the Elder Days. He could no longer attribute to his Elves, sober and lore-wise as they had become, the lighthearted and almost animistic cosmology of the 'Lost Tales'. Originally, Middle-earth was lit by two great Lamps, overthrown by Melkor, the original Dark Lord, in the war that drove the Valar into the furthest West; there they made the Two Trees, Telperion and Laurelin, of which the Moon and Sun were merely the last posthumous flower and fruit, respectively. All this, Tolkien felt, had to go. In 1948 he wrote a 'Round Earth' version of the *Ainulindalë*, just as an experiment in the kind of drastic revision that the whole legendarium would require if the Elves followed the Copernican astronomy. He then seems to have written a new 'Flat Earth' version, labelling the 1930s draft (Christopher Tolkien's 'B' text) the 'Old Flat Earth' version.

Both the new texts were sent to Katherine Farrer, who much preferred the 'Flat Earth' version. It is indeed more richly and strongly imagined, and of course much better integrated with the tales of *The Silmarillion* as a whole, because it had grown up with them. For the time, Tolkien seems to have accepted her judgement as a sound one. But after *The Lord of the Rings* was finished, and still more after it was published, he kept returning to the question of the round Earth and the intractable facts about the Sun. However imaginatively satisfying was the idea of the Sun as the fruit of Laurelin, he felt that it simply would not do:

> At that point (in reconsideration of the early cosmogonic parts) I was inclined to adhere to the Flat Earth and the astronomically absurd business of making the Sun and Moon. But you can make up stories of that kind when you live among people who have the same general background of imagination, when the Sun 'really' rises in the East and goes down in the West, etc. When however (no matter how little most people know or think about astronomy) it is the general belief that we live upon a 'spherical' island in 'Space' you cannot do this any more.
>
> One loses, of course, the dramatic impact of such things as the first 'incarnates' waking in a starlit world – or the coming of the High Elves to Middle-earth and unfurling their banners at the *first* rising of the Moon.

As his son observes, Tolkien 'was devising – from within it – a fearful weapon against his own creation'. He never completed the revision to his satisfaction, and perhaps it never could have been done. Too much else would have had to come out along with it. But even if he retained the primitive story of the Sun and Moon, it was becoming obvious to him that other parts of the *Silmarillion* needed serious reconsideration.

One of these was the notion that Men first appeared in Middle-earth at the creation of the Sun. Another document in *Morgoth's Ring*, quite finished and several times revised, is the *Athrabeth Finrod ah Andreth*, a discussion between the Elven-king Finrod Felagund and a mortal wise-woman on the nature of human and Elvish death and the ultimate fate of both races. In the first draft, Andreth offered a florid and rather brassy account of the Fall of Man, not incompatible with the story in Genesis except in detail, but very different in tone. It could easily have come out of a Rider Haggard novel – or out of something like *Animal Farm*. The burden of the tale is that dealing with the Devil is like paying Danegeld: he not only breaks his promises, but raises his price the next time, until in the end you give him everything for nothing. In the revision he cut all this out, feeling that it was 'too like a parody of Christianity'. But it remained clear that the 300 years between the rising of the Sun and the coming of the Edain into the West was not nearly enough for the long and tragic history that Men must already have behind them. In rough revisions of the chronology, he pushed the advent of Men far into the past, even before the era when the Elves first went to Valinor.

For late in life, Tolkien was concerned not only to reconcile the myths with one another and with Copernicus, but with Catholic theology as well. He remained convinced that the overt mention of religious practices had no place in fantasy, or at least the kind of Secondary World fantasy he was writing; but he became painfully scrupulous about making the theological speculations of Finrod and Andreth dovetail with the teachings of the Church. In the end this, too, failed of any satisfactory solution. I am convinced that the unproductiveness of his last years was not caused by age alone, but by his growing realization that he had set himself an impossible task. He was trying to fit too many things together in too small a compass, and, fatally, he had already published too much. He had already worked on the legendarium for nearly forty years when *The Lord of the Rings* was published. If he had been assured of forty more years of working life, he might have been able to reconstruct the entire *Silmarillion* on the more serious and theological basis he had come to envision, and still maintain 'backwards compatibility' with *The Hobbit* and *The Lord of the Rings*. But for an old man, conscious of fading powers and the imminence of death, it was too much.

WHAT IS ELF?

Tolkien was fond of saying that he invented the whole apparatus and history of Middle-earth in order to have a place in which *Elen síla lumenn' omentielvo* would be a common greeting. By the time he finished *The Lord of the Rings,* if not long before, he had pre-eminently achieved that goal. What checked him at that point, and indeed largely stymied his creative talents for the remainder of his life, was a close inquiry into what sort of creatures these were who greeted one another in this way. He could never find a satisfactory answer to the question: *What is an Elf?* Even his agonized abandonment of the 'Flat Earth' cosmology of *The Silmarillion* was conditioned by this question. He had come to believe that the Elves were too wise to invent, and too truthful to tell, stories about their past that obviously contradicted the astronomical facts.

So what is an Elf? The existing folklore concerning elves is most unhelpful. One source describes them as beings of unearthly grace and beauty; another, as soulless and heartless tricksters who will blithely destroy any human being who stumbles in their way; still another, as the spawn of Cain. The word *elf* goes back with little change to primitive Germanic, in which it means approximately 'Pale One' (it comes from the same root as Latin *albus* and English *albino*); but the old Germanic tales that have come down to us are singularly unenlightening. The Anglo-

Saxons had evidently a lively belief, or at least interest, in elves, but seemed to find it unprofitable or unpropitious to tell stories about them. Not even the Norsemen had much to say about them. Most of the interest in elves, in a purely literary sense, is much later, and belongs largely to the German tradition of *Märchen*. Here is Tolkien, in a letter to Rayner Unwin dated 1961:

> There are no songs or stories preserved about Elves or Dwarfs in ancient English, and little enough in any other Germanic language. Words, a few names, that is about all. I do not recall any Dwarf or Elf that plays an actual part in any story save Andvari in the Norse versions of the Nibelung matter. There is no story attached to the name Eikinskjaldi, save the one that I invented for Thorin Oakenshield. As far as old English goes 'dwarf' (*dweorg*) is a mere gloss for *nanus*, or the name of convulsions and recurrent fevers; and 'elf' we should suppose to be associated only with rheumatism, toothache and nightmares, if it were not for the occurrence of *ælfsciene* 'elven-fair' applied to Sarah and Judith!, and a few glosses such as *dryades, wudu-elfen*. In all Old English poetry 'elves' (*ylfe*) occurs once only, in *Beowulf*, associated with trolls, giants, and the Undead, as the accursed offspring of Cain. The gap between that and, say, Elrond or Galadriel is not bridged by learning.

That gap is a pretty puzzle. Tolkien seems to have begun conventionally enough, with twee phantasies of twinkle-toed Wee Folk supping on dewdrops and sleeping in buttercups. His early poem 'Goblin Feet' is a vile enough example of the degraded 'elfy-welfy' tradition he soon came to despise:

> *The air is full of wings*
> *Of the blundering beetle-things*
> *That go droning by a-whirring and a-humming.*
> *O! I hear the tiny horns*

Of enchanted leprechauns
And the padded feet of many gnomes a-coming.

O! the lights! O! the gleams: O! the little tinkling sounds:
O! the rustle of their noiseless little robes:
O! the echo of their feet, of their little happy feet;
O! their swinging lamps in little star-lit globes.

I could quote more, but this is the point at which, in Dorothy Parker's immortal phrase, 'Tonstant Weader fwowed up.'

Fortunately, Tolkien's friends severely criticized this and others of his early poems, and probably contributed much to the skill and *gravitas* he was to show in *The Book of Lost Tales*. (In the end the *gravitas* became almost too grave to bear, but a movement in that direction was certainly called for.) G. B. Smith, who was killed in the Somme not long after, seems to have been particularly instrumental in persuading Tolkien to this change of style. If so, Smith deserves to be recognized as one of the most influential literary critics of the last century. Tolkien's other close friends, Christopher Wiseman and R. Q. Gilson, naturally shared in this salutary process.

In the *Lost Tales*, Tolkien seems to have adopted the idea that Elves *nowadays* were the tiny fairies of Victorian fancy, reduced by long 'fading', whereas Men had grown larger; but in the Elder Days they had been much alike in stature. In the end he entirely rejected the layer of accretion on the 'Matter' of the Elves that made them diminutive and vapid. But it was a long road. Even in *The Hobbit*, he could still make his Elves sing this kind of rubbish:

O! What are you doing,
And where are you going?
Your ponies need shoeing!
The river is flowing!
O! tra-la-la-lally
here down in the valley!

By 1954 he had abandoned all that, and wrote to Naomi Mitchison:

> 'Elves' is a translation, not perhaps now very suitable, but originally good enough, of *Quendi*. . . . I should say that they represent really Men with greatly enhanced creative and aesthetic faculties, greater beauty and longer life, and nobility.

In this late conception, which few other fantasy authors have had the philosophical or theological background to appreciate or copy, Tolkien's Elves were a representation of Unfallen Man, or of a race close akin to Men who had escaped the taint of original sin. Much of the difference between the two kindreds was held to arise from what in Judaeo-Christian legend is termed the fall of Adam.

In his late work, Tolkien sometimes went to ridiculous lengths to emphasize the 'unfallenness' of the Elves. Galadriel, in some of his last essays, is almost a surrogate for the Virgin Mary. The *Athrabeth Finrod ah Andreth* was not so far gone; it represented perhaps the fullest exposition of the *philosophical* implications of telling stories about Elves, without going overboard and losing the *narrative* element. After that Tolkien wrote many essays but very little fiction as such.

There is another element in the elves of folklore that Tolkien seized upon avidly and expanded into a major theme of his work. The elves are said to be infinitely artistic and creative, lovers of beauty, singers of songs with magical power. A man may stray into the revels of the elves for a night, only to find a hundred years gone when he returns to his people in the morning. (The peculiar dilation of time in Lothlórien was an expression of this motif.) Hearing the horns of Elfland may inspire mortals to the purest love or the greatest courage, or it may drive them mad with *Sehnsucht*. The art of the elves, particularly Tolkien's Elves, is so powerful, and so directly experienced, that it can unseat the reason of mortals. We are not strong enough for it. Tolkien did not make full use of this theme in his fiction, but he enlarged upon it in his essay 'On Fairy-Stories':

Now 'Faërian Drama' – those plays which according to abundant records the elves have often presented to men – can produce Fantasy with a realism and immediacy beyond the compass of any human mechanism. As a result their usual effect (upon a man) is to go beyond Secondary Belief. If you are present at a Faërian drama you yourself are, or think you are, bodily inside its Secondary World. The experience may be very similar to Dreaming and has (it would seem) sometimes (by men) been confounded with it. But in Faërian drama you are in a dream that some other mind is weaving, and the knowledge of that alarming fact may slip from your grasp. To experience *directly* a Secondary World: the potion is too strong, and you give to it Primary Belief, however marvellous the events. You are deluded – whether that is the intention of the elves (always or at any time) is another question. They at any rate are not themselves deluded. This is for them a form of Art, and distinct from Wizardry or Magic, properly so called.

In this essay, Tolkien has a disturbing tendency to discuss the Elves as if they were real; though he gently pricks the bubble of his own Secondary World, created in the space of a few paragraphs for rhetorical effect, on the following page:

> To the elvish craft, Enchantment, Fantasy aspires.... Of this desire the elves, in their better (but still perilous) part, are made; and it is from them that we may learn what is the central desire and aspiration of human Fantasy – even if the elves are, all the more in so far as they are, only a product of Fantasy itself.

This art of Enchantment, or Faërian Drama, crops up in all kinds of contexts that have apparently nothing to do with Elves: it is a deep-seated, perhaps a fundamental, human desire. The interest in telepathy – not in 'mind-reading', but in the ability to *send* one's thoughts directly to another without the clumsy and distorting medium of language – is perhaps a manifestation of that desire. And illusions of the sort that Tolkien would call 'enchanted' occur in other kinds of fiction than pure fantasy. They are quite common in science fiction. Virtual Reality is the usual modern term. But even in the 'Golden Age' and before, the wish was there. Stanley G. Weinbaum made a Faërian drama, or a counterfeit of one, the central conceit in one of his tongue-in-cheek Van Manderpootz stories; and the Visi-Sonor, that strange musical instrument which has so important a function in the plot of Asimov's *Foundation and Empire,* has virtually the same effect. Oddly enough, Tolkien does not make much use of this particular device in his own fiction. He does so twice, I believe, in *The Lord of the Rings,* but in neither case is the 'dramatist' an Elf. Frodo has strange visions out of the past in response to the tales told by Tom Bombadil, and later on, in Rivendell, he has a similar experience while Bilbo is reciting 'Eärendil was a mariner'. It is an Elvish art in origin, apparently, but other 'speaking peoples' are not incapable of learning it.

Since Tolkien's death, a new conception of Elves has arisen in popular culture, partly derived from him, partly from his imitators, but above all from *Dungeons & Dragons.* The Perilous Realm became Fantasyland, and Elves became part of the furniture. As is rather appropriate in a game built almost entirely on the adolescent-wish-fulfilment elements of fantasy, D&D-style Elves are usually portrayed as eternal adolescents, physically beautiful and alluring, *ex officio* Good People who nevertheless seem not to have much conscience or to feel the need of any. They take their name from Tolkien, but their character from Peter Pan. Diana Wynne Jones has a shot at these in *The Tough Guide to Fantasyland:*

> Elves appear to have deteriorated generally since the coming of humans. If you meet Elves, expect to have to listen for hours while they tell you about this – many Elves are great bores on the subject – and about what glories there were in ancient days. They will intersperse their account with nostalgic ditties (*songs of aching beauty*) and conclude by telling you how great numbers of Elves have become so wearied with the thinning of the old golden wonders that they have all departed, departed into

the West. This is correct, provided you take it with the understanding that Elves do not say anything quite straight. Many
Elves have indeed gone West, to Minnesota and thence to Cali-
fornia, where they have great fun wearing punk clothes and rid-
ing motorbikes.

The fundamental flippancy and immaturity of the latter-day treatment of Elves has, I think, never been skewered more aptly.

Nowadays there seem to be four schools of thought in dealing with
Elves. The one school, the D&D school, the up-to-date teenage elfy-welfy
school, has really nothing to say about its subject matter; but then, it has
precious little to say about anything. This stuff is pure escapist fiction, in
the worst sense of the word: it escapes *from* humdrum modern life without escaping *to* anywhere but the grotesque Utopia of *World of Warcraft*
and other online games. The escape is as much from genuine fantasy as it
is from reality. The second school, to which Moorcock and Miéville and
their friends are greatly devoted, considers Elves a horrible manifestation of childishness and artistic ineptitude, and goes to great lengths to
make its not-quite-human races as unlike them as possible. Sometimes
they stoop to parody. Moorcock's Melnibonéans could be described as
a kind of anti-Elves, for instance, retaining much of the physical appearance of post-Tolkienian Elves while turning them into agents of the most
unenlightened evil.

The third school carries on the tradition of the 19th-century German
Elves more or less without any Tolkienian influence at all. Poul Ander-
son was perhaps the most influential member of that school; his most
important work on Elves was done before *The Lord of the Rings* was
published. Perhaps the most adept, or at any rate, the most *famous* and
adept member of that school is Susanna Clarke. The Gentleman with the
Thistledown Hair is clearly an Elf of the amoral kind straight out of German folklore, though the word is never applied to him in the text. He is
the sort of person that you refer to, if you must mention him at all, as one
of the Fair Folk, lest he should hear and take offence: just as the Greeks
used to butter up the Furies by calling them *Eumenides*.

The fourth school simply shirks the question by writing about something else entirely. This is a productive and honourable approach, but it will not teach us anything about Elves; so I pass it over.

It seems to me that Tolkien's Elves represented something more than any of these latter-day schools are equipped to deal with; something valuable, something it behooves us to examine more closely. The nature of the *Quendi* is closely bound up with Tolkien's deeply Catholic understanding of good and evil, and the influence of this can be seen in his imitators and detractors. D&D Elves are automatically pigeonholed on the side of Good – 'Chaotic Good' to be precise, an oxymoron that would probably have made Tolkien physically sick. The vacuity of the 'alignment' system in D&D is faithfully reflected in, or itself reflects, the moral disengagement of much modern fantasy.

The strands of Elvendom converged into the bright tapestry of Tolkien, and have diverged in rags and tatters since. To me, at least, as a latecomer to the Catholic faith that Tolkien embraced all his intellectual life, the idea of Elves as *unfallen* Men had an irresistible fascination. It seemed to me that one could make all kinds of inquiries into the nature of Good and Evil by postulating a race of otherwise human people who could always distinguish the good and followed it as by instinct. It also seemed to me that Tolkien had done very little of this. Lewis did something like it in *Out of the Silent Planet,* with its brilliant climax in which the pompous rhetoric of self-justification by Fallen Man is translated into the bald condemnation of the angelic language:

> Weston accepted the arrangement at once. He believed that the hour of his death was come and he was determined to utter the thing – almost the only thing outside his own science – which he had to say. He cleared his throat, almost he struck a gesture, and began:
>
> 'To you I may seem a vulgar robber, but I bear on my shoulders the destiny of the human race. Your tribal life with its stone-age weapons and beehive huts, its primitive coracles and elementary social structure, has nothing to compare with

our civilization – with our science, medicine and law, our armies, our architecture, our commerce, and our transport system which is rapidly annihilating space and time. Our right to supersede you is the right of the higher over the lower. Life–'

'Half a moment,' said Ransom in English. 'That's about as much as I can manage at one go.' Then, turning to Oyarsa, he began translating as well as he could. The process was difficult and the result – which he felt to be rather unsatisfactory – was something like this:

'Among us, Oyarsa, there is a kind of *hnau* who will take other *hnaus'* food and – and things, when they are not looking. He says he is not an ordinary one of that kind. He says what he does now will make very different things happen to those of our people who are not yet born. He says that, among you, *hnau* of one kindred live all together and the *hrossa* have spears like those we used a very long time ago and your huts are small and round and your boats small and light like our old ones, and you have one ruler. He says it is different with us. He says we know much. There is a thing happens in our world when the body of a living creature feels pains and becomes weak, and he says we sometimes know how to stop it. He says we have many bent people and we kill them or shut them in huts and that we have people for settling quarrels between the bent *hnau* about their huts and mates and things. He says we have many ways for the *hnau* of one land to kill those of another and some are trained to do it. He says we build very big and strong huts of stones and other things – like the *pfifltriggi*. And he says we exchange many things among ourselves and can carry heavy weights very quickly a long way. Because of all this, he says it would not be the act of a bent *hnau* if our people killed all your people.'

Granting, if only for argument's sake, that the Fall really occurred, how much of human pride, human social structure, even human technology, is the product of that Fall and not of our essential nature? Our three great legacies from the ancient world, forming the plinth on which almost the whole of Western civilization has been built, are Greek philosophy, Jewish religion, and Roman law. Greek philosophy strove to find Man's place in the universe, to recover a more accurate sense of right and wrong, and to purify the reasoning faculty of errors and corrupt influences. Judaism sought to restore the relationship of Man to his Creator, and to instruct Man in his moral and prudential duties. Roman law was designed to punish those who harmed society by transgressing the moral code, to arbitrate disputes between people who could not be counted upon to recognize each other's rights or even to tell the truth, and above all, to rule an empire wisely even when the rulers themselves were maniacal fools.

All three are admirable and audacious efforts to deal with the consequences of the Fall, but it was the Fall that made them necessary, and the Fall still renders them insufficient. Our own distinctive addition to the sum of human knowledge, Western science, has in some respects made matters worse: it increases our capacity both to do evil and to survive it, which encourages us to tolerate it. No ancient society could have withstood the sufferings and massacres that rulers like Hitler, Stalin, and Mao inflicted on their own (and other) peoples; but then, no ancient society could have inflicted such things. As Huxley said (and Tolkien quoted), ours is an age of improved means to deteriorated ends.

It is easy to see that a society of perfect people would not have philosophy, religion, or law in anything like the forms we know. What else would change? Supposing the Elves to be immortal, which is correct according to folklore, their political systems would be drastically different as well. Mark Twain once wrote that the best form of government would be rule by a perfectly just and capable autocrat; but since a perfect autocrat must die, and be replaced by an imperfect successor, autocracy is not the best but the very worst form of government. Succession would scarcely be a problem in a society of immortals. States and nations might tend to form around dominating personalities, and disappear if the ruler was slain or incapacitated: much as political factions in republican Rome were not permanent political parties, but temporary alliances of individuals or families. Of course, so many of the functions of a human state would be unnecessary that we should hardly think of an Elvish autocracy as a government at all.

Now, *pace* Tolkien, the Elves of folklore are much more ambiguous morally than his ideal of Unfallen Man. The Tolkien Method, if we apply it sincerely, requires us to try and reconcile such paradoxes before we start throwing away individual elements. There are at least two ways that Elvish ethics would differ from ours, and both would tend to make the actions of the Elves seem heartless and even monstrous to short-lived humans.

First, anyone with the kind of easy moral clarity that Tolkien attributed to his Elves, and that Christian theology suggests will be universal among redeemed and glorified humans, would naturally appear judgemental and arbitrary to those less enlightened. The idea of righteousness has gone clean out of favour in our own society, and anyone with clear notions of right and wrong is labelled *self-righteous* instead. This naturally follows if you accept the axiom that all morals are relative, and that each person is free to invent his own standards of good and evil. In that case, righteousness is a thing that can only be applied by and to the self. But if there is some objective standard – which we must grant, by the terms of the argument: if there was a Fall, we fell *from* somewhere, from a state that was by definition better than any of us enjoy now – then to be simply righteous, without self-aggrandizement or self-regard, is possible at least in principle.

Nothing makes us fallen humans angry quicker than the spectacle of someone not only professing but following a stricter moral standard than we ourselves care to adopt. It shakes our complacency and damages our self-conceit, and if long endured, makes us ashamed that we expect so little of ourselves (and deliver even less). In America before the Civil War, slaveholders hated and cursed the Abolitionists, not because the abolition of slavery was wrong, but because at bottom they knew that it was right. They wanted to feel that they were good and moral people, but they also wanted to keep their slaves; and Abolitionism forced them to choose. They wanted to be good, but not *that* good. Plato once speculated at length on what would happen if a genuinely good man came among ordinary humans. He concluded that, unable to ignore his superior standards and unwilling to live up to them, they would turn on him in outrage, curse him, torture him, and murder him. Four hundred years later, the people of Judaea proved him right.

But there is another respect in which an 'unfallen' morality would be inferior to our own. It would be intolerant of mistakes: not in the sense of disapproving them, but of not having any method of dealing with them at all. It is clumsy people who learn how to fall without hurting themselves, because they fall so often; the naturally graceful have a harder time of it. In ethics there are any number of what are sometimes called secondary virtues, which can only operate in response to evils. You cannot show courage, for instance, until you face danger and fear. Even perfect humans would have need of courage, because no matter how much you improve man himself, his environment is still a dangerous place. But other virtues, formed in reaction to specifically moral evils, would scarcely exist. In a society of perfect people there would be no forgiveness, because no one would give offence. There would be no tolerance, because there would be no disagreeable actions to tolerate. There would be no pity, because there would be no undeserved suffering. And there would probably not be even a word for mercy, because nobody would have need of it. Mercy can almost be defined as treating people more kindly than they deserve; it would have no meaning if everyone deserved the best of treatment all the time. In such a society, if someone did choose to do an evil deed, his neighbours would probably react with horror and shock, and leave him to suffer the consequences of his own actions. They would not have enough experience of evil-doing to have learnt any other response. And the attitude of these perfect people towards us ordinary fallen humans would probably be rather like the attitude of the King of Brobdingnag when Gulliver told him about gunpowder.

Imagine, if you can, what it would be like to have a neighbour whose judgement in both ethical and prudential matters was honed by a thousand years of experience; who never neglected a duty or transgressed another's rights; who could not understand how anyone might be ignorant enough to do evil by accident, or wilful enough to do it on purpose; and whose own choices took into account, not only the needs of the moment, but the consequences she and her loved ones might face centuries in the future. I think most of us would find such a neighbour priggish, arbitrary, stiff-necked, and given to the most bizarre snap judgements; and many of us would not tolerate her for long. And the lower our own ethical standards, the less we would be able to understand hers. Perhaps our ancestors used to accuse the Elves of being soulless, not because the elves lacked conscience, but because they had more than mere mortals could easily comprehend. Tolkien at least adumbrated such a process, when he made the Rohirrim regard the Elves with superstitious fear. They saw Lothlórien, or 'Dwimordene', as a place of ill omen, and Galadriel as a terrible sorceress. The frequent presence of 'Elf-friends', particularly Wizards and the Men of Gondor, must have modified this idea pretty heavily; Aragorn, in particular, taught the Rohirrim a good lesson about the perils of misjudging their neighbours. So far as the published work goes, Tolkien toyed with this idea rather than explored it.

All this is idle speculation, of course, as touches reality – though it may do us good now and then to contemplate the idea of higher standards than we now possess. But it is at any rate a sufficiently exotic idea to use in a work of fantasy; and to use more thoroughly than Tolkien had time or room for. I think it more interesting than any of the other answers yet proposed to the question, 'What is an Elf?' I believe it has enormous satiric potential, just as Swift's Brobdingnagians and Lewis's Malacandrians had, and much as Jesus, with his consistently radical use of the *a fortiori*, held up a ruthless mirror to the conventional morality of his own day.

This style of fantasy, it seems to me, might be considered a sort of science fiction where the sciences involved are theology and ethics. Both of these fields were indeed considered sciences in a more contemplative age; indeed, theology was once called the Queen of the Sciences before she was dethroned and replaced by mathematics.

The extraordinary success of technological instruments in expanding our knowledge of the physical sciences has given most of us, scientists not excepted, a vague idea that science is concerned only with what our instruments can measure. But psychology, which has unquestionably attained the status of a science, depends not only on standardized tests and EEGs, but on human beings' subjective and unquantifiable reports of their own states of mind. Biology depends not only on DNA analysis and the dissection of specimens, but on observing living things in their own habitat. If we set out to observe a living God in his own habitat, as it were, and observe him (the only way we can) through the lens of our own subjective experience, we must not expect the kind of precise and quantitative results obtained by physicists; but we can still approach the subject in a scientific frame of mind, and do our best with the evidence available to us. The modern denigration of theology is based not so much on a refusal to speculate as on a refusal even to observe.

It is true that there is more divergence of opinion about theology than about physics; this is at least partly because the study of theology, having been long neglected, is less advanced than the study of physics, and also because most people are ignorant even of the theological knowledge that we do have. At one time, natural philosophers fought battles of nearly religious intensity over the questions whether the planets followed circular orbits or elliptical ones, and whether light was made up of waves or particles. In the first case, they decided definitely which alternative was correct; in the second, they found that both were useful but deficient, like the blind men's impressions of the elephant. The instrumental proofs came later; sometimes, indeed, until the true explanations were accepted *ex hypothesi,* the instruments themselves could not be invented. The theoretical basis for their existence was assumed in building them, and the fact that they worked was the evidence that it was correct.

But one useful device is equally available to physicists and theologians, and that is the thought-experiment. It was the thought-experiments of Einstein that chiefly led him to his two theories of relativity, and not all the laboratories and instruments in the world could have helped him do it. It is at least possible that theological thought-experiments might produce enlightening results; and it is certain that ethical thought-experiments can do so, for half the world's fiction consists of ethical thought-experiments of greater or lesser degrees of subtlety. The story of Spider-Man is in part an inquiry into good; the story of Humbert Humbert is an inquiry into evil. (I am among the heretics who find more value in the former.) Tennyson's King Arthur was invented to examine the fate of a good man undone by the evil men around him; Donaldson's Thomas Covenant was the reverse, an evil man, or at least a deeply flawed one, redeemed by the good people he discovered in the Land. And to return to Tolkien, Frodo is a good person tested to destruction by hardship and temptation. We must always be leery of accepting these experiments at face value, for it is all too easy for an author to measure the results with his thumb on the scales; but they can still be of use to us. I think most people have learnt important lessons from fiction, in one medium or another. Some of the lessons were even true.

So how might a writer today go about applying this technique in the 'Matter' of the Elves? Perhaps I may be permitted to give an example from my own work. I have always been fascinated by the claim in Genesis that it was the very first humans who sinned, even before they had time to breed, so that all their offspring carried the resulting taint. Supposing that one wanted to postulate the existence of sinless humans alongside the kind we know and are, what easier way than to defer Original Sin to the second generation? It was from this that I developed the myth of Dân, the Adam-figure of my own Secondary World, and the differing fates of his three sons. The protagonist of *The Eye of the Maker*, a young fellow of iconoclastic bent, recounts the tale in potted form:

> 'Yes, I've heard the story. Dân was made by the Maker in his own image, whatever that means, and Eia, the first woman, in the first days of Färinor. They had three sons, Färon, Morak, and Vardan. The Destroyer spoke to each of them out of the void. Färon sent him marching with a flea in his ear, but Morak listened to him and rebelled against the Maker; Vardan stayed out of the quarrel. Morak killed his father, raped his mother, and sired the Morakh on her. I forget the rest, but it was all very sordid and mythological.'

The idea is that Färon, who remained unfallen, became the ancestor of the *Färinoth*, whom it is very indelicate, not to say unlucky, to call Elves: just as it seems to be with Clarke's Gentleman with the Thistledown Hair, if not for precisely the same reasons. As with the Furies, it is precisely the justice of the Fair Folk that men fear.

Morak's descendants owe something to the 'goblin tradition' from which Tolkien derived the Orcs, something to trolls and ogres, and something to the old psychological theories about Neanderthal man founded on his apparent incapacity to make representational art. We feel, perhaps rightly, that the creation of art is the most uniquely and characteristically human activity, and the one in which we most nearly resemble God (or gods); and Tolkien made the creativity of the Elves their most strikingly superhuman feature.

Vardan, whose descendants were mortal men like ourselves, did not sell his soul outright; his sin, like Adam's, was to think that he could be his own master and do without God. In the event, the Maker generally, if sorrowfully, respected the wish of Vardan's people to be independent and find their own way, but the Destroyer interfered with them shamelessly. This is the peril of all would-be neutrals, as the Belgians found out in both World Wars. So said Screwtape:

> The humans are always putting up claims to ownership which sound equally funny in Heaven and in Hell. . . . They will find out in the end, never fear, to whom their time, their souls, and their bodies really belong – certainly not to them, whatever happens. At present the Enemy says 'Mine' of everything on the pedantic, legalistic ground that He made it; Our Father hopes in the end to say 'Mine' of all things on the more realistic and dynamic ground of conquest.

And so you have my own answer to a question that lies very near the heart of modern fantasy. My answer is the Fair Folk whose good seems to us more terrible than our evil, whose love seems more heartless than our hatred, whose art seems more real than our reality; whose knowledge seems like folly to us in our ignorance; who grieve at the wickedness of mortals, but leave us to the fate we chose for ourselves; and who have no word for mercy, for they have no need of it.

THE TERMINAL ORC

If the powers of Morgoth and the nature of the Elves gave Tolkien endless trouble in preparing *The Silmarillion* for publication, the problem of the Orcs nearly frightened him into giving up the attempt. How this happened sheds light on some interesting facets of Tolkien's creative process, the mentality of his critics, and the ethics of fantasy in general.

C. S. Lewis famously said that nobody could influence Tolkien – 'you might as well try to influence a Bandersnatch' – but in fact this was not true. Tolkien's mind soaked up influences like a sponge, and he nearly always had a strong reaction to criticism, especially adverse criticism. What you could not do was influence him in a direction of your choosing, or predict how your criticism would affect him.

In *The Lays of Beleriand,* there is an exceptionally interesting section in which Lewis dissected the first thousand-odd lines of Tolkien's immensely long (and never finished) *Lay of Leithian.* Lewis was a superbly able literary critic, but his poetic talents (which were considerable) did not tend in the same direction as Tolkien's at all. Lewis's forte was the English poetry of the sixteenth century and thereabouts, on which he was one of the world's leading authorities, as Tolkien was on Old and Middle English. If he had had a closer affinity with Tolkien's muse, his criticism might have been immensely destructive. Instead he followed his own ear for verse, and the emendations he suggested were almost invariably unsuited to Tolkien's style. Tolkien could accept the criticisms without any temptation to adopt the suggested verses. A typical example occurs in lines 123–126. Here are Tolkien's original lines:

> *swift ruin red of fire and sword*
> *leapt forth on all denied his word,*
> *and all the lands beyond the hills*
> *were filled with sorrow and with ills.*

Lewis objected, and rightly, to the omission of *that* from the second line in order to salvage the metre:

> The relative understood. I suspect both the construction and the word *denied,* neither of which has the true ring. H reads:

> *And ruin red of fire and sword*
> *To all that would not hail him lord*
> *Came fast, and far beyond the hills*
> *Spread Northern wail and iron ills.*

This is better, perhaps, but it is not Tolkien. He must have snorted vigorously at 'Northern wail and iron ills' when he read it. Tolkien was an exceptionally 'tough-minded' author, in the original sense of the word: that is, he was concerned not with vague generalities, but with specific and concrete details, and would not be bamboozled by plausible handwaving. Lewis's phrase is emotionally strong but literally meaningless. The criticism was valid, but the suggested cure was worse than the disease. When Tolkien revised the poem in light of Lewis's comments, he rewrote the lines this way:

> *With fire and sword his ruin red*
> *on all that would not bow the head*

like lightning fell. The Northern land
lay groaning neath his ghastly hand.

This removes the original difficulty without introducing a lot of clap-trap about directional crying and sick metal. *Neath* is slightly precious, a quality Tolkien had not yet fully outgrown, though he had come far since the days of 'Goblin Feet'. In the late 1940s, after receiving another detailed and strenuous criticism of the *Lay*, Tolkien returned to it and substantially rewrote the opening and various other sections. The lines that correspond to those above reached this final form:

Slowly his shadow like a cloud
rolled from the North, and on the proud
that would not yield his vengeance fell;
to death or thraldom under hell
all things he doomed: the Northern land
lay cowed beneath his ghastly hand.

So the affectation of *neath* and the borderline cliché of *ruin red* are purged.

After *The Lord of the Rings* was published, Tolkien received some let-ters from readers of a theological bent, good Catholics or at least good Christians, who objected strongly to some details about the Elves and Orcs. In particular they objected to the idea, then present in Tolkien's unpublished (but privately circulated) texts, that the Elves were subject to reincarnation if slain. Tolkien at first gave them short shrift, saying that even if reincarnation was not a mode employed by God in *this* world, that did not make it inconceivable that He might use it in *another* world, on creatures not strictly human. But in the end he re-examined the whole question of Elvish incarnation, decided that it did not bear close scrutiny, and threw the idea out. For those Elves who had necessarily (because it was already established in the published tales) to return from the halls of

Mandos, he posited a mechanism analogous to the resurrection of the dead in Christian doctrine.

The problem of the Orcs was not so easily resolved. In 1954, Peter Hastings, manager of a Catholic bookshop in Oxford, wrote to Tolkien suggesting that he had 'overstepped the mark in metaphysical matters'. Most of his objections had in fact already been dealt with in work that Hastings had not yet read, but he put his finger on the one that would never be adequately resolved: the origin of the Orcs. He did not believe that evil could create, and still less could it create living creatures with self-awareness and souls; and he was among those who were disturbed by the idea of a rational incarnate creature that appeared to be totally irredeemable. Tolkien replied, in part:

> Treebeard does not say that the Dark Lord 'created' Trolls and Orcs. He says he 'made' them in *counterfeit* of certain creatures pre-existing. There is, to me, a wide gulf between the two statements, so wide that Treebeard's statement could (in my world) have possibly been true. It is *not* true actually of the Orcs – who are fundamentally a race of 'rational incarnate' creatures, though horribly corrupted, if no more so than many Men to be met today. . . .
>
> Suffering and experience (and possibly the Ring itself) gave Frodo more insight; and you will read in Ch. I of Book VI the words to Sam. 'The Shadow that bred them can only mock, it cannot make real new things of its own. I don't think it gave life to the Orcs, it only ruined them and twisted them.'

This answer contented Tolkien for that time, and it seems to have contented Mr. Hastings. But the objections kept coming from other quarters. Why would God (or, to give him his Elvish name, Eru) *permit* the Dark Lord to so degrade God's children that they would pass beyond the reach of redemption or even of conscience? Tolkien tried various ways to answer that, but none quite satisfied him. At one point he experimented with the idea that the Orcs were *animals,* perhaps with an admixture of Elvish or Mannish genetic material, bred by Morgoth until they were sufficiently intelligent to have the power of speech and to at least mimic some of the operations of human thought. Or perhaps they were biological automatons, in the state Tolkien envisioned for the Dwarves before Eru gave them true life: puppets of their maker, moved only by his will, and collapsing into insensate matter when his power was removed from them. But that would not explain how the Orcs could fight among themselves. Clearly Tolkien was influenced here by his private critics, if not by his public ones. He was influenced almost to the point of paralysis; his creative faculties very nearly dried up.

In fact, the Orcs represent a detail of the Problem of Evil that Tolkien never quite brought himself to face. This problem has dogged humans since the beginning of recorded history, and probably longer, and we have been shirking it just as long. If you care to accept the account in the Book of Genesis, both the problem and the shirking began when Adam and Eve ate the forbidden fruit, and Adam blamed Eve and Eve blamed the serpent. Both were particularly acute in the twentieth century, and above all in the age of horrors that encompassed the two World Wars. Trench warfare, poison gas, concentration camps, massacres, Communism, Fascism, the OGPU and Gestapo, the Rape of Nanking, Munich, the Nazi-Soviet Pact, Barbarossa, Pearl Harbor, Auschwitz, Dresden, Hiroshima: these are not the extraordinary things of that epoch, but the entirely typical ones. As William Golding put it in his essay 'Fable':

> I must say that anyone who passed through those years without understanding that man produces evil as a bee produces honey, must have been blind or wrong in the head.

This sounds like opinion, but it is a reasonably precise statement of fact. To any great danger, a human being can have one of three responses: fight, flight, or surrender. Anybody can list the ways that citizens and statesmen, nations and cultures, responded to the crises of those days. Authors and artists did the same, less directly, through the medium of their work.

Ezra Pound surrendered by doing barefaced propaganda for the Nazis, and was almost hanged as a war criminal. Bertolt Brecht was luckier in his choice of masters: he surrendered to Stalin, and the Soviet régime kept him physically safe until he died. Sartre surrendered, not to any particular dictator, but in general; he 'solved' the problem of Evil by denying the existence of Good. According to his brand of existentialism, the only thing that mattered was 'self-affirmation' in the face of a meaningless universe. If you saw a beggar in the street and gave him money, that was one way to affirm your own existence; if you ran him over on purpose with your car, that was another way; and one affirmation was just as good as the other. 'Wrong-headed' is surely a rather mild way to describe such a philosophy.

Others chose flight, which in those days meant making themselves blind to nearly everything that was going on around them. James Joyce sat out the First World War in the safety of neutral Switzerland, writing an obsessively detailed book about an insurance salesman in Dublin in 1904. As the next war approached, Henry Miller proclaimed himself indifferent to the impending fall of Western civilization, and dived joyfully into a wallow of mysticism and pornography. In between, the nineteen-twenties were the heyday of 'Art for Art's sake'. As Orwell said in 'Inside the Whale':

> Our eyes are directed to Rome, to Byzantium, to Montparnasse, to Mexico, to the Etruscans, to the subconscious, to the solar plexus – to everywhere except the places where things are actually happening.

J. R. R. Tolkien chose to fight.

Some philosophers have tried to fight by constructing purely naturalistic systems of ethics that would somehow account for and incorporate the moral intuitions that most humans have in common. Of these, Stoicism was the most successful in ancient times; in modern times, Utilitarianism. But none of these attempts really succeeded, for they did not take the fight to the hottest part of the battleground. Most of us will accept certain ethical propositions as matters of principle, when we are safe and comfortable and have no difficult decisions to make. But as soon as it becomes difficult to follow the rules, our courage fails us. We flinch from the fight, we make exceptions and excuses, and retire from the field behind a smokescreen of casuistry.

What all the great secular systems of ethics have in common (apart from their content, in which all of them are remarkably similar) is the fewness of their followers. It takes considerable intelligence, education, and willpower to be a successful Stoic, or Utilitarian, or to live strictly by the ethical precepts of Confucius or Buddha. In a sense it is true that Good can be identified with enlightened self-interest; the trouble is that so very few people are enlightened. Most of us do not have the intellectual prowess for that kind of enlightenment, and those who need it most do not even desire it.

Napoleon spoke of 'two o'clock in the morning courage', the cold courage that is trained into a man's bones and will allow him to act bravely in no matter what adversity. Hardly anybody is born with such courage, and most people never acquire it. To truly follow a purely secular ethical code we need two o'clock in the morning enlightenment: the ability to see, through the clamour of our desires and fears, what is the wise thing to do in each situation we encounter. And we need the courage as well, or we will not be able to go through with some of the actions we know are necessary. But we need to have a good-sized portion of enlightenment before we can even understand the need to be enlightened. Not many of us get that far without the sanctions of some religion or other. In this sense it is quite true that the fear of God is the beginning of wisdom. It is not the only possible beginning, but even today it remains the usual one.

Worse yet, there is always the retreat into Existentialism or nihilism. If there is not a God, or some other force that gives the moral law a basis for objective existence, we can solve the Problem of Evil by wishing it away. Many modern persons – I have known a fair collection – deny the existence of evil, which means also denying the existence of good. It is very fashionable to talk about 'shades of grey', and castigate others for 'black-and-white' thinking. To a certain degree this is a valid criticism.

But many persons talk and act as if everything were the *same* shade of grey. This can only be true in one circumstance. Some men wear black hats, and some wear white hats; but all hats are grey in the dark. This solution reminds me of a moderately old joke:

> Q. How many Microsoft programmers does it take to change a lightbulb?
> A. None. Bill Gates defined darkness as the industry standard.

If you take it for granted that all humans will follow their basest impulses, you need not worry about the Problem of Evil. But then you have to worry about the Problem of Good, for in fact people have an annoyingly persistent way of acting according to something that can only be called conscience. We so often do what is right, even when it is not expedient; and still more often we *wish* to do what is right, and fail to do it, and feel ashamed. There is a kind of shame that has nothing to do with morality. A man may boast about how fast he can run, and feel ashamed when he loses a foot-race. That is easy to explain. We all feel ashamed when we lose face before our peers. But when a man who makes no boast does a thing he believes to be wrong, he feels ashamed even when nobody catches him. He loses no face, except to himself; but that is enough. He desires goodness as the other man desires speed; and any theory of ethics or psychology that does not account for this desire is hopelessly incomplete.

There are some people, it is true, who do not desire goodness, and who have no evident capacity to feel ashamed of their actions as long as their actions are successful. A man who loves speed will not feel ashamed of winning a race, unless he has done it by cheating. A sociopath who loves speed will not be ashamed no matter how he wins. I have known a number of sociopaths, including one who was successfully treated and apparently cured; you might say I have had an opportunity to examine the Orcish mindset firsthand. The problem of the Orcs is not so theoretical as Tolkien's critics made out, and Tolkien might have profited by examining some of our Orc-like brothers and sisters himself.

There are two close portrayals of Orcs in *The Lord of the Rings*. The second, the encounter between Shagrat and Gorbag outside Shelob's lair, is a masterpiece of satire. These two Orcs are not quite sociopaths, for they have moral standards of a kind; they are just comically incapable, as Shippey points out, of applying them to their own actions. After the Orcs capture the unconscious Frodo, one of their captains makes a clearly moralizing remark to the other:

> 'It's my guess you won't find much in that little fellow,' said Gorbag. 'He may have had nothing to do with the real mischief. The big fellow with the sharp sword doesn't seem to have thought him worth much anyhow – just left him lying: regular elvish trick.'

Regular elvish trick: in other words, the sort of thing the enemy does, but that *our* side would never stoop to. There is no denying that he disapproves of abandoning one's comrades in that way. But Shagrat knows something Gorbag does not: Frodo isn't dead!

> 'Garn!' said Shagrat. 'She's got more than one poison. When she's hunting, she just gives 'em a dab in the neck and they go limp as boned fish, and then she has her way with them. D'you remember old Ufthak? We lost him for days. Then we found him in a corner; hanging up he was, but he was wide awake and glaring. How we laughed! She'd forgotten him, maybe, but we didn't touch him – no good interfering with Her.'

As Shippey observes: 'What can one say but "regular orcish trick"?' And Gorbag, who was quick enough to disapprove of Sam's abandoning Frodo, has no word to say against Shagrat for abandoning Ufthak. Instead he starts joking about all the jolly psychological tortures he can put Frodo through without violating the letter of Sauron's order that all captives are to be kept safe and intact. Orcs have morals; they just happen to be coupled with a hypocrisy so perfect that it is essentially unconscious.

Morals are a stick to beat their enemies with, never a ruler to measure their own behaviour.

The other major appearance of individual Orcs occurs earlier in *The Two Towers,* when the Uruk-hai capture Merry and Pippin. This chapter sheds less light on Orcish ethics, but it does let fall one beam that shines fairly on the target:

> 'My dear tender little fools,' hissed Grishnákh, 'everything you have, and everything you know, will be got out of you in due time.... What do you think you've been kept alive for? My dear little fellows, please believe me when I say that it was not out of kindness: that's not even one of Uglúk's faults.'

Most of us, probably, have met persons who talked like that. We speak of being kind to a fault, but it is not difficult to find people who think kindness is always and in itself a fault. There are those who think kindness is merely a form of weakness, and that if you do not choose to inflict suffering on others, it is only because you lack the strength to do so, or at best because you are busy with other things. In his reply to Peter Hastings, Tolkien points out that his Trolls, too, lack the faculty of kindness or pity, even though they temporarily refrain from doing Bilbo all the harm they might do:

> I might not (if *The Hobbit* had been more carefully written, and my world so much thought about 20 years ago) have used the expression 'poor little blighter', just as I should not have called the troll *William.* But I discerned no pity even then, and put in a plain caveat. Pity must restrain one from doing something immediately desirable and seemingly advantageous. There is no more 'pity' here than in a beast of prey yawning, or lazily patting a creature it could eat, but does not want to, since it is not hungry. Or indeed than there is in many of men's actions, whose real roots are in satiety, sloth, or a purely non-moral natural softness, though they may dignify them by 'pity's' name.

I have known men and women with exactly that kind of non-moral natural softness, who would not hurt a fly, not because they have any pity for flies, but merely because they get no pleasure and see no advantage in doing so. And I have known some who did get pleasure from cruelty, and though I could not say it of my own knowledge, I am sure some of them picked the wings off flies. If they did not, it was because they had moved on to bigger game.

The genuine sociopath, however, while still remaining a full member of the human species, goes one step further than Tolkien's Orcs. Sociopaths as a rule do not even use moral standards as a stick to beat their (absent) enemies with. They do not disapprove of the evil that others do, but of the softness and weakness that others show when they refrain from doing evil. 'You should have kicked him when he was down' is about as close to a moral judgement as some of them ever come. Of course they have learnt to mimic the language of morality and even of contrition, because they know that it is an effective way to manipulate the emotions of others. All successful sociopaths are manipulative. A human being cannot live entirely alone, except by overwhelming effort and stern asceticism, neither of which commends itself to the sociopathic mind. And if you are to live among people, you must either have a genuine fellow-feeling for them, or be able to fool them into doing your will. Mark Twain patterned Huckleberry Finn's father after one of the town drunkards in the Hannibal of his boyhood, and portrayed the technique with lapidary precision:

> When he got out the new judge said he was a-going to make a man of him. . . . After supper he talked to him about temperance and such things till the old man cried, and said he'd been a fool, and fooled away his life; but now he was a-going to turn over a new leaf and be a man nobody wouldn't be ashamed of, and he hoped the judge would help him and not look down on him. The judge said he could hug him for them words; so *he* cried, and his wife she cried again; pap said he'd been a man

that had always been misunderstood before, and the judge said he believed it. . . .

Then they tucked the old man into a beautiful room, which was the spare room, and in the night some time he got powerful thirsty and clumb out on to the porch-roof and slid down a stanchion and traded his new coat for a jug of forty-rod, and clumb back again and had a good old time. . . . And when they come to look at that spare room they had to take soundings before they could navigate it.

The judge he felt kind of sore. He said he reckoned a body could reform the old man with a shotgun, maybe, but he didn't know no other way.

Old Finn was a fine example of a sociopath. He said a lot of phrases that had no meaning to him, simply because he knew the judge wanted to hear them, and he got a bed for the night and a new suit of clothes out of it; the clothes were swappable for whisky; the bed, once he had slept, furnished him the amusement of wrecking it. One could venture the hypothesis that his alcoholism had destroyed the faculty of empathy in him, either through brain damage directly, or because his craving for drink was so strong that he would do anything to satisfy it. But it is highly probable that he never had much of that faculty in the first place.

We know that certain kinds of brain injury can induce sociopathy or states similar to it. Prefrontal lobotomy, that fine psychiatric treatment from the Age of Horrors, often produced radical changes of personality in its victims. One often reported was a loss of empathy and conscience. Fortunately, a still more common effect of lobotomy was listlessness and loss of initiative. A person without a conscience is little danger to others if she has not the energy to go out and damage them.

But more specific techniques were developed for destroying small portions of the prefrontal lobe, in the hopes (never quite fulfilled) of producing particular changes in behaviour. It would in principle be possible to permanently damage the part of the brain responsible for the sense of moral obligation without taking away the subject's energy and initiative.

Michael Crichton's early novel *The Terminal Man* postulates just such an operation. When that story begins, Harry Benson is already suffering from an acute disinhibitory lesion, which is a real and recognized form of brain injury; it causes him to have episodes of random violence, with amnesia afterwards. He is treated by inserting electrodes into the brain, so that selected neurons can be stimulated to damp out the impulses caused by the lesion. Of course, since Crichton was a technological horror writer by trade, the operation subtly fails and ends up making matters much worse, turning Benson into a serial killer. This is a worst-case scenario, but a possible one; Crichton did his homework on the medical issues involved. A variant of the procedure is actually used today as a treatment for severe depression in certain patients who do not respond to medication, but the specific electrical stimulus used, and the part of the brain to which it is applied, make it impossible to produce the kind of Jekyll-and-Hyde side-effect that Crichton portrayed.

Now, if a carefully plotted alteration to the brain can produce a Terminal Man, why not a Terminal Orc? Saruman seems to have been a genetic engineer of sorts: it is fairly clear that he cross-bred Men with Orcs, producing hybrids like Bill Ferny's friend at Bree, the 'squint-eyed southerner', and also the Uruks of Isengard who could endure full daylight. One can easily imagine that Morgoth had the power (and his minions the skill) to alter the genes of Men or even Elves in such a way that the prefrontal lobe would develop abnormally. The brain of such a modified Man simply would not contain the centre where most of our moral awareness takes place; he might be as incapable as any sociopath of developing a conscience. This is a horrifying thought, but hardly more so than the forced lobotomization of thousands in our own history. That was going on in the years when Tolkien was writing *The Lord of the Rings*, and although of course it never turned humans into Orcs, it did quite often make them more Orc-like.

Tolkien came in for a good deal of criticism from Christian readers for making the Orcs intrinsically evil, either without souls, or with souls permanently fallen and incapable of being saved. This is probably an unfair criticism, though Tolkien felt the force of it in his last years, and tried hard to answer it. Perhaps there is no good answer. But he can at least be acquitted of the specifically theological charge against him. It was said that God would never permit anyone to produce a race of sentient beings that were naturally and incurably evil. But God has already permitted us to produce individual humans of a very similar kind.

It is a very difficult thing to save the soul of a sociopath, or even to explain the idea of souls to one. The cured sociopath whom I knew was treated by carefully and rationally teaching him the value of seeking mutual benefit in his interactions with others. He came to understand that it was more profitable, and a lot less dangerous, to barter with people than simply to take advantage of them. (The dangers were obvious, for at least two people had tried to kill him. It was this, he told me, that made him seek treatment and change his way of living.) In trying to think of what he might offer them in exchange for the things he wanted, he grew to have some appreciation of other people's wants and needs, and some of the capacity for empathy that he had never developed by nature. If it was not empathy that he developed, it was a calculated and habitual imitation of it, and that may be a distinction without a difference. But as far as I know, he never took up any kind of religious belief, though he adopted elements of Zen philosophy and practised some techniques of meditation. The idea of the soul, let alone the Christian idea of saving it, was, I believe, a closed book to him.

On a less intractable level – the level of software rather than hardware, as we say nowadays – there has been a whole movement to deprive people of their moral compass by teaching them from childhood that all moral standards are merely expressions of personal emotion, that they are not binding on anyone and have no general validity. Lewis wrote at length about this movement in *The Abolition of Man,* and I will not repeat his arguments here. It is sufficient to say that education, too, can do much to make Men into Orcs. It would no doubt be possible to combine methods. My friend the ex-sociopath was able to overcome his dysfunction because he was carefully taught the principles of ethics in terms that his mind could accept and understand. But if some Dark Lord or White Wizard began to breed potential sociopaths on purpose, and then reared them in a culture designed to keep them from all knowledge of ethics, it would be very difficult indeed to rescue them from Orc-hood.

Difficult, but perhaps not impossible. One thing that Tolkien's detractors on this point tend to forget is that in Middle-earth in the Third Age, *no one's* soul was saved. By setting his story in a remote period of our own past, at least as an imaginative conceit, he also set it in a period where the Christian salvation he devoutly believed in had not yet come to pass. Even the best of his mortal characters – Hobbits, Rohirrim, Men of Gondor – were in effect virtuous pagans, vaguely aware (as were the Stoics) of the existence of God, but having no theology, no sacred texts, no traditions of worship. Their homage to Eru was tendered in a purely negative manner, by resisting the shadow of Sauron with all their might – or else it was not, as in the case of Denethor. As for Elves, Dwarves, and Wizards, they did not have souls in the technical Christian sense of the word.

So what then of the Orcs? They were as pagan as the Men of the Third Age, but decidedly not virtuous. Yet if Morgoth and Sauron had corrupted them into that form of body and mind, their lack of virtue was not their own fault but the fault of their corrupters. Some theologians, and some religions, say that God judges souls according to the use they have made of their opportunities. Tolkien believed as much. Let us, then, try to look at the Orcs from something like his theological point of view. Perhaps there were Orcs who had vague stirrings of real conscience, who actually tried sometimes not to do the things they scorned as 'typical elvish tricks'. Perhaps there were Orcs who were better than Heinrich Himmler, or even as saintly as Al Capone. If so, they might have been rewarded according to their measure; there might even be a sort of Heaven for Orcs who did what little they could to resist the evil of their masters. But it would be a long and tedious job to housebreak an Orc's soul for paradise. The Orcish version of Purgatory is not a place I would ever wish to see.

WRITING DOWN THE DRAGON

Sir, if you made verse you would doubt symbols.
I am afraid of the little loosed dragons.
When the means are autonomous, they are deadly;
   when words
escape from verse they hurry to rape souls;
when sensation slips from intellect, expect the tyrant;
the brood of carriers levels the good they carry.
—Charles Williams, Taliessin Through Logres

Men have conceived not only of elves, but they have imagined gods, and worshipped them, even worshipped those most deformed by their authors' own evil. But they have made false gods out of other materials: their notions, their banners, their monies; even their sciences and their social and economic theories have demanded human sacrifice.
—Tolkien, 'On Fairy-Stories'

The 'little loosed dragons' are, of course, coins of King Arthur's realm, stamped with the dragon as an emblem of the House of Pendragon. Williams' Arthurian poems were largely outside the range of Tolkien's sympathy, but when C. S. Lewis quoted these lines approvingly, Tolkien must have emphatically agreed. The danger of divorcing means from their proper ends runs all through the works and thoughts of the Inklings. Notions and banners, money and science, have each their idolatrous devotees, who take a useful means and turn it into an end in itself – an idol demanding of sacrifice, and often human sacrifice. As for social and economic theories, the very word *ideology* can be roughly defined as 'taking one moral principle, forsaking all others, and then following it off a cliff'. Marx made a god of economic equality; the Social Darwinists made a god of economic liberty; the Eugenicists, like Lewis's villain Weston, made the love of kindred 'a little blind Oyarsa', with calamitous results. In each case, their followers took a thing that was good in its place and used it to destroy more important and fundamental goods – on which the good they worshipped always turned out to depend.

In mediaeval Christendom, the dragon was often regarded as a symbol of the Devil. This interpretation goes back to St. John's seven-headed monster in Revelation, and was powerfully encouraged by the legend of St. George. But it can hardly be said that Christianity damaged the reputation of the worm. The ancient Greeks, who gave us the word *dragon*, had little good to say of dragon-kind. There was Python, the dragon of Delphi, a grim chthonic creature that was the sworn enemy of Apollo (who slew him), and apparently no friend of man. The Ismenian Dragon was said to be the offspring of Ares, which right away gives it a bad character; it was killed by Cadmus, and even its teeth, when Cadmus planted them, grew into such bloodthirsty warriors that they immediately began killing one another until only five were left. Then you have the Colchian Dragon, which guarded the Golden Fleece, and Ladon, who guarded the Golden Apples of the Hesperides: evidently dragons have always liked to guard golden things. Dragons, or beasts like them, occur in still earlier tales out of Babylon and points eastward; and if those tales end happily, it is because the hero has slain the beast.

At some point in the long history of the dragon, it wormed its way into the myths of the ancient North. We shall probably never know exactly when or why. Dragons are tolerably common currency in Norse mythology, but like Elves, they exist mostly in the background; few of the surviving narratives actually feature a dragon. In fact, as Tolkien pointed out, we have only two stories *about* dragons from the whole Northern tradition; and in both, true to form, the dragon is duly slain. Iceland preserved the *Völsunga saga,* in which Sigurd kills Fáfnir; England preserved *Beowulf,* whose hero kills a dragon that does not even receive the dignity of a name. Tolkien did not think much of the latter, but he returned time and again to Fáfnir. He retold the whole story in verse, as *The Legend of Sigurd and Gudrún;* but what is more to our purpose, he used Fáfnir as the model for two of the most vivid dragons in modern literature.

Fáfnir, as the *Völsunga saga* tells us, was originally a dwarf, one of the three sons of Hreidmar. His brother Ótr was a skin-changer (as Tolkien's Beorn would call it), who took the form of an otter by day: hence his name. Ótr was killed and skinned by Loki – who else? – who then came round to Hreidmar's own house, with Odin and Hœnir for company, to show off his catch. Hreidmar took the three gods captive and demanded a were-gild for his son; Loki paid him off in the tainted coin of Andvari's cursed gold. In due course Fáfnir killed his father to get the gold, and turned into a dragon in his greed to guard it. (C. S. Lewis pinched the idea for *The Voyage of the Dawn Treader,* in which Eustace Scrubb is turned into a dragon by sleeping on a dead dragon's hoard and claiming the gold for himself.) Thereafter Fáfnir lived in the ordinary way of dragons, until his surviving brother, Regin, trained up Sigurd to be his bane. Fáfnir was not a *winged* dragon; Sigurd caught him by digging a hole in his path and stabbing him from underneath as he passed.

These are the bare facts of the case; but Tolkien uses them with great cunning and inventiveness. By the time he is finished, it is a Norse tale no longer, but Tolkien's; or rather, it is several of Tolkien's tales, together with some allusions to stories not fully told. He first delved into this material in the *Lost Tales,* in 'Turambar and the Foalókë', which (among other things) marries portions of the Sigurd legend to the Finnish tale of Kullervo. This story went through more than the usual number of re-writings and re-imaginings, and eventually appeared as Chapter 21 of *The*

Silmarillion. Years later, Christopher Tolkien compiled the longest and fullest versions and published them as *The Children of Húrin*; but that book, while of course more detailed, does not contradict the *Silmarillion* text on any important point, so for simplicity I shall cite the *Silmarillion* version here.

First there is the matter of Regin. As a young man, Túrin runs away from his foster father, the elven-king Thingol, and takes up with a band of outlaws. His men come upon three Dwarves, killing one with an arrow as he flees, and capturing another. The captive leads the outlaws to his home, an ancient Dwarvish stronghold inside a hill, now all but abandoned, and ransoms himself by letting them use it as their lair; and he names the place Bar-en-Danwedh, the House of Ransom. But the Dwarf whom Túrin's men killed was Khîm, the captive's son, whose corpse has been brought home by his brother:

> Then pity rose in Túrin's heart, and he said to Mîm: 'Alas! I would recall that shaft, if I could. Now Bar-en-Danwedh this house shall be called in truth; and if ever I come to any wealth, I will pay you a ransom of gold for your son, in token of sorrow, though it gladden your heart no more.'

In terms of the sources, the captive Dwarf takes the role of Hreidmar, and his dead son that of Ótr; but Túrin's pity puts him on a higher moral plane than the Æsir, or at least Loki. He never actually pays a ransom for Khîm's death, but the captive takes the intention for the deed; and in the end the Dwarf will come into great wealth, though as in the original, there is a curse on the gold, and he will get no good out of it.

After the first meeting, however, the Dwarf puts aside the role of Hreidmar, and loosely takes up that of Regin – though in a different way. Regin was Sigurd's foster-father; Tolkien's Dwarf was only Túrin's unwilling host.

The fullest modern version of the Sigurd legend is of course Wagner's Ring cycle. There the role of Regin is taken over by Mime, who brings up Siegfried and trains him in the skills he will need to conquer the dragon.

Siegfried despises his foster-father all the same, and in fact Mime is not a very attractive character. It is not unreasonable to call Siegfried ungrateful; at any rate Tolkien must have thought so, for he made *his* Regin-figure a treacherous and repulsive figure throughout, and took away his role as the hero's teacher. In the *Lost Tales,* the Dwarves are a naturally evil people. Tolkien abandoned this idea in the next phase of the legends, but this one character was too firmly established to be changed; so he invented the idea that he was a renegade Dwarf, one of a mean and degenerate people, banished from the great Dwarf-cities of the Blue Mountains. And in one of his few definite borrowings from Wagner, he fastened on this character the name of Mîm, the Petty-dwarf. He deserves it better than Wagner's Mime did: he lives down to his reputation. He betrays Túrin's band to the Orcs; Túrin is captured, and all his men are slain.

So (we may say) Hreidmar, Ótr, and Regin are represented in Tolkien's version by Mîm, Khîm, and Mîm again, respectively. (Ibun is not so much a character as a pallbearer.) It is entirely typical of Tolkien's method that he abstracts the deeds out of the old legends and distributes them among the characters in his own way. What is more, Fáfnir is not part of this family. Tolkien's dragon is not a Dwarf transformed by magic, but a dragon by origin: Glaurung, first of the Urulóki, the father of all dragons. Glaurung has played a minor part in the tale so far, serving as a kind of heavy artillery in support of Morgoth's Orcs. Now he takes the stage as one of Morgoth's leading servants.

In Glaurung, the means have not yet become autonomous, but they are deadly all the same. Glaurung represents what we may call 'the dragon in service': he acts throughout on the express orders of Morgoth, stage-managing the fulfilment of Morgoth's curse against Túrin and his sister. He is an implacable and pitiless foe, though he can take in unwary mortals with an expert imitation of pity. In Glaurung, Tolkien gives full narrative development to several dragonish powers that are used to less effect in the old tales.

After his misadventure among the Petty-dwarves, Túrin is rescued and becomes a great captain in the Elvish city of Nargothrond. Too great: for his victories reveal him to Morgoth again, and the Dark Lord sends Orcs and the dragon to destroy the city, with the dragon pretty definitely in command. Here Tolkien uses the motif of the dragon's spell, interpreted as a kind of super-hypnosis. The worm can hold his victims spellbound by the power of his eyes (as snakes are said to do to small birds) and of his voice, and can implant post-hypnotic suggestions in their minds that they will unswervingly obey, in some cases, for years thereafter. While Nargothrond is sacked by the Orcs and the captive Elves are led away, Glaurung immobilizes Túrin and teaches him self-hatred:

> Glaurung spoke again, taunting Túrin, and he said: 'Evil have been all thy ways, son of Húrin. Thankless fosterling, outlaw, slayer of thy friend, thief of love, usurper of Nargothrond, captain foolhardy, and deserter of thy kin. As thralls thy mother and thy sister live in Dor-lómin, in misery and want. Thou art arrayed as a prince, but they go in rags; and for thee they yearn, but thou carest not for that. Glad may thy father be to learn that he hath such a son; as learn he shall.' And Túrin being under the spell of Glaurung hearkened to his words, and he saw himself as in a mirror misshapen by malice, and loathed that which he saw.
>
> And while he was yet held by the eyes of the dragon in torment of mind, and could not stir, the Orcs drove away the herded captives, and they passed nigh to Túrin and crossed over the bridge. Among them was Finduilas, and she cried out to Túrin as she went; but not until her cries and the wailing of the captives was lost upon the northward road did Glaurung release Túrin, and he might not stop his ears against that voice that haunted him after.

Glaurung's spell sends Túrin on a wild-goose chase back to Dor-lómin, trying to rescue his mother and sister. In fact they had fled from that country long before, seizing the interval of safety that Túrin himself created by his martial exploits. The dragon's tale is a cruel lie – doubly cruel, because while Túrin wastes his time trying to save his kin, the Orcs kill his beloved, the Elf-princess Finduilas. On his return from Dor-lómin he falls in with the Men of Brethil, who are hard pressed by Orcs, and helps them win a hard-fought victory; from them he learns Finduilas's fate. The dragon's spell is broken, too late to avert any of the harm it has done, or mend it.

Glaurung uses this power to still greater and more tragic effect. Morwen and Niënor leave their refuge, against counsel, to find Túrin; and Niënor falls into the power of Glaurung. On her he casts a spell of total forgetfulness; her amnesia is so profound that she even forgets how to speak, and has to be taught language again. Such spells are common enough in folk-tales, and fit well with the magic of the dragon as Tolkien has so far employed it; but so far as I know, Tolkien himself was the first to combine the two in this way. In this case the spell endures until Glaurung's own death breaks it. Túrin has never met Niënor – he was sent away to King Thingol about the time she was born. When he finds her in the wilderness, aimless and witless, she is to him the image of the lost Finduilas; he takes her to Brethil, falls in love with her, and duly marries her. So the motif of the hero's unwitting incest with his sister, which Tolkien took from the Kullervo tale, becomes an effect of the dragon's spell upon them both.

A dragon would hardly be a dragon if he did not come to a bad end; and Glaurung's end, fittingly enough, comes at Túrin's hands. Here again we have the touch of Fáfnir: Túrin lies in wait for the dragon in a narrow ravine, and kills him with a sword-thrust in the belly while Glaurung is crossing overhead. But Tolkien is not done with Glaurung and his power yet. As the dragon lies dying, he puts a spell on Túrin with his eyes, sending him into a cataleptic swoon; and the upshot of the whole encounter is that Túrin and Niënor each commit suicide believing the other to be already dead. It is perhaps the most perfect and pitiless tragedy in all of modern fantasy, on a par with *Oedipus Rex.*

The genesis of the Túrin tale, then, lies in Tolkien's more or less arbitrary decision to combine elements of the two tales of Sigurd and Kullervo. The disparity of the two produces a 'crux', which Tolkien resolves by incorporating divers magical motifs into the spell of the dragon's gaze.

The rest is a matter of detail, and since this is Tolkien, the details are worked out with meticulous precision, the fruit of more than fifty years' work. And the engine of the plot – Glaurung, the *diabolus ex machina* – emerges as Tolkien's most vivid and compelling portrait of merciless and *detailed* evil. The dragon fulfils Morgoth's curse by getting inside the heroes' heads, circumscribing their actions in such a way that even his own death does not give them any way of escape.

In the writings on Middle-earth, Tolkien refers to two more dragons by name, but so far as the published books go, they are scarcely more than names, brought in to add the appearance of depth. One is Ancalagon the Black, who appears briefly in *The Silmarillion* as Morgoth's ultimate weapon, who wreaked havoc on the host of the Valar, and smashed the mountains of Thangorodrim to ruins when he fell. Ancalagon was killed by Eärendil with the help of the Eagles, and if Tolkien had ever written any long form of the Eärendil story, we should probably have heard more about him. As it is, we have only the brief mention in the last chapter of *The Silmarillion,* and Gandalf's observation in *The Lord of the Rings:* 'nor was there ever any dragon, not even Ancalagon the Black, who could have harmed the One Ring'. The other is Scatha, who was killed by an ancestor of Eorl the Young; the Horn of Rohan is said to have come from Scatha's hoard.

In *The Hobbit,* the Dwarves discuss

> dragon-slayings historical, dubious, and mythical, and the various sorts of stabs and jabs and undercuts, and the different arts, devices and stratagems by which they had been accomplished.

Within the story, this could refer to the deaths of Glaurung, Ancalagon, and Scatha, and perhaps other dragons not named. Outside of the story, it certainly refers to the death of Beowulf's dragon and of Fáfnir. 'Stabs and jabs and undercuts' is a good description of the methods employed in those five cases. But none of these methods are much good against a *flying* dragon, not while he is airborne; and this brings us to the most famous of Tolkien's dragons, who met his end in quite a different way.

If Glaurung represents the dragon in service, Smaug is the independent dragon, in whom the means have become autonomous. Smaug is capable of great cunning and a kind of cruel amusement, and he can be influenced by flattery; but in true dragonish style, his only real motive is greed. He destroyed the Dwarf-kingdom of Erebor and the Mannish kingdom of Dale, for no better reason than to steal their treasure and hoard it; and when he had lain upon that bed of gold and jewels for a century and a half, without ever making any other use of it, he could still be roused to burning rage by discovering that a single golden cup had been stolen from under him. The incident of the stolen cup comes, of course, from *Beowulf.* The psychology of the miser comes from real life, whetted to a keen satirical edge by Tolkien's skill:

> Dragons may not have much real use for all their wealth, but they know it to an ounce as a rule, especially after long possession; and Smaug was no exception. . . . Then he missed the cup!
>
> Thieves! Fire! Murder! Such a thing had not happened since first he came to the Mountain! His rage passes description – the sort of rage that is only seen when rich folk that have more than they can enjoy suddenly lose something that they have long had but never before used or wanted.

There is not much room for doubt as to what kind of 'rich folk' Tolkien had in mind. As Tom Shippey has observed, Smaug's speaking style is taken from the British upper classes of the earlier twentieth century: not the old-blood aristocracy, which had lost much of its wealth by Tolkien's time, and was losing even its political clout, but the titled parvenus, the sons or grandsons of self-made men, who went to public schools and Oxbridge to learn the manners of aristocrats. Such men were plutocrats pure and simple, but by adopting the camouflage of the nobility they managed to get themselves respected and even admired by snobs and social climbers. They mastered the difficult art – an art seldom practised outside England – of being utterly obsessed with making money while never actually talking about it and pretending not to care about it.

In his talk with Bilbo, Smaug plays the aristocrat – that kind of aristocrat – to perfection. He feigns indifference to his treasure: 'Come along! Help yourself again, there is plenty and to spare!' And while he is tickled by Bilbo's attempts at flattery, he is still more offended by his effrontery. One does not walk into a dragon's parlour (or a life peer's) and strike up a conversation without a proper introduction. Smaug, in the fashion of his class, points up Bilbo's gaucherie and cuts him with an artfully worded hint:

> 'You have nice manners for a thief and a liar,' said the dragon. 'You seem familiar with my name, but I don't seem to remember smelling you before.'

Familiar: the ultimate insult from a member of the Upper Crust to a social inferior. One does not presume to be *familiar* with one's betters. As Tom Shippey has observed, it is exactly the note of a colonel in a first-class railway carriage, rebuffing an unwanted attempt at conversation with freezing hauteur. But Smaug is not 'to the manner born': he is a thief and a liar himself, and if he has any point of superiority to a wealthy and respectable gentlehobbit, it is that he is a thief on the grand scale. When Bilbo refuses to be put off, Smaug drops his false colours and talks frankly about the business angle:

> 'I suppose you got a fair price for that cup last night?' he went on. 'Come now, did you? Nothing at all! Well, that's just like them. And I suppose they are skulking outside, and your job is to do all the dangerous work and get what you can when I'm not looking – for them? And you will get a fair share? Don't you believe it! If you get off alive, you will be lucky.'
>
> Bilbo was now beginning to feel really uncomfortable. Whenever Smaug's roving eye, seeking for him in the shadows,

flashed across him, he trembled, and an unaccountable desire seized hold of him to rush out and reveal himself and tell all the truth to Smaug. In fact he was in grievous danger of coming under the dragon-spell.

As Tolkien puts it with masterly understatement, 'Smaug had rather an overwhelming personality.' It is the same trick that Glaurung used on Túrin. But Glaurung was in the service of Morgoth, and the instrument of Morgoth's curse; Smaug is in nobody's service but his own. The means are autonomous, and therefore deadly; but because they *are* autonomous, they are also resistible. Smaug is not a creature with a mind and a heart that have been corrupted by greed; he *is* greed – a spirit of pure avarice, which happens to have come into possession of a mind and a heart, and a rather formidable body, and uses them merely as weapons. He has never experienced, can hardly even imagine, any other motive than greed; so he leaves Bilbo's strongest desires out of account, and the spell miscarries. To make matters worse, he lets Bilbo get away with a vital bit of information: Smaug has a weakness – a bare patch in his underbelly, 'as bare as a snail out of its shell'. It is this weakness that allows Bard the bowman to slay the worm with a single arrow (though evidently a magic one), in lieu of the usual 'stabs and jabs and undercuts'. It all began with Smaug's fearful miscalculation of his enemy's motives. A dragon acting under orders, we may surmise, would never have made such elementary mistakes.

And yet; and yet. Sauron himself, who (as the Necromancer) was claiming to be vicegerent of Morgoth at this time, and (in his own name) would soon claim to be Morgoth himself, made a more sophisticated version of the same error, to his infinite cost. Sauron, says Gandalf, 'is very wise, and weighs all things to a nicety in the scales of his malice. But the only measure that he knows is desire, desire for power.' This is a more subtle and adaptable measure than the mere desire for gold; power-lust can understand gold-lust, for wealth is a form of power, but gold-lust has a very hard time understanding power-lust. It is always easier to apply a general idea to a specific case than to extend a specific idea to cover the general case. But even the general case of power-lust falls far short of explaining the whole range of human motives. Sam Gamgee's motives were so far beyond Sauron's range that he could not even tempt him. When the Ring gave Sam visions of unlimited power, he only laughed and went on about his business.

Sauron is not a dragon, of course, but he stands in the same relation to power-lust as a dragon to gold-lust: its chief devotee and exemplar, a spirit so wasted and simplified that he has lost knowledge of any other motive. Tolkien employed the resonance of names very cleverly here. He always insisted, and we must take his word (and the word of his various Elvish dictionaries), that the name *Sauron* does not come from Greek *sauros* 'lizard', but from an Elvish root **thaw-, *thawra,* meaning 'detestable'. The character makes his first appearance in the 1920s under the Gnomish name *Thû*, which is derived from **thaw-* according to the normal rules of Gnomish phonetic change. At some point Tolkien decided that Primitive Elvish *th-* becomes *s-* in Quenya. The suffix *-on*, used in Quenya to form nouns, was established at an early date. So Gnomish *Thû* = Quenya *Sauron*. This name first appears in *The Lost Road,* and with it, the idea that Morgoth's principal lieutenant survived his master's fall to wreak havoc in the later ages of Middle-earth. Tolkien could have stuck with *Thû* instead (or the later Sindarin equivalent, *Gorthaur*). But 'Sauron' is a much nastier-sounding name, much more suitable to a Dark Lord. It not only reminds one of the Greek *sauros*, and of impressive and dangerous things like dinosaurs; it also contains the sound of the English word *sour*. *Sauron* naturally replaced *Thû* for much the same reason that *Morgoth* replaced the original name *Melko*. The name was not derived from the Greek word for lizard, but Tolkien was no fool, and was glad to take advantage of the coincidence.

So you have Sauron the Necromancer, the successor to Morgoth as Dark Lord; but where Morgoth tried to dominate Middle-earth by brute force, the much weaker Sauron had to do it by subversion. The Elven-rings were his perfect instruments, for he had a hand in their making, and made sure they were suitable for his purpose. First he helped the Elves make the lesser rings; then he made the One Ring to subvert the other rings; then he took the lesser rings by force, and gave them out as gifts to various kings and rulers, and so subverted them. He was well on his way to subverting all of Middle-earth before the Last Alliance stopped him.

Each kind or subset of the Rings had its own peculiar powers, specifically designed to tempt one of the peoples of Middle-earth by appealing to their basest desire. With the Elves he could not do much; all they wanted to do was keep Middle-earth as it was, a kind of park or pleasance in which they could live with their memories of the old great days. The Three Rings, accordingly, had the power to preserve things, to stave off the ravages of time: powers not even remotely evil in themselves, though they could tempt the Elves to resist good when it came in the form of change. Men, being mortal, desired to be free from death, and being highly social creatures, desired power over their kin; these were desires that Sauron thoroughly understood and could easily corrupt.

The Dwarves loved jewels and precious metals, not merely as things to collect and hoard, but as raw materials from which they could make things of great beauty. The Seven Rings that Sauron gave them became the foundation of the seven great treasure-hoards of the Dwarf-lords. We do not actually know that the Rings helped the Dwarves grow richer; perhaps they only made them more greedy and possessive, so that they kept their gold instead of spending or giving it freely. It is another instance of the dragonish impulse at work. In the old Norse legend, Andvari got hold of a magic ring and used it to gain a golden treasure; then Fáfnir got the ring and the treasure, and turned into a dragon in his greed to guard them. Tolkien's Dwarves went through a similar process. Sauron gave them their Rings; they accumulated the treasures; then their wealth attracted dragons, who slew the Dwarves or drove them off and squatted on the gold. Four of the Seven Rings, we are told, were consumed by dragons: probably the most perfect food ever devised for a dragonish appetite. As the old saying runs, *Serpens nisi serpentem comederit draco non fit* – 'Unless a serpent eats another serpent, he does not become a dragon.' We may surmise that eating one of the Seven Rings was the equivalent of swallowing a dragon in pill form.

The complex enmity between Dwarves and dragons has deep roots both in the internal history of Middle-earth and in our own history and folklore. It touches something fundamental about the human desire (and need) for material goods. Each of Tolkien's major non-human or semi-human races exemplifies and exaggerates a particular trait very near the heart of human nature. Elves reflect our artistic nature. Orcs reflect our nature as fallen beings – moral agents who do not live up to our own standards. Dwarves reflect us as economic beings, and dragons, on this plan, represent or reify the economic urge when it gains autonomy – when we stop desiring wealth as a means and desire it as an end in itself.

If we think of them in this way, the real-life analogues of dragons are not hard to find. We do not have the power to create living creatures and pour our undiluted avarice into them; but we can create virtual bodies, and equate them with persons (for certain purposes) by a legal figment. This invention was one of the glories of the Middle Ages; it was done by a magical document known as a charter, and the process of creating the body, logically enough, was called incorporation. In Western Christendom from about the twelfth century on, there was a positive mania for creating corporate entities. The jurists of those times were, by and large, not fools, so they did not grant corporations the right to marry, for instance, or the right to vote (in places and times where voting occurred); but they had the right to make contracts, to be landlords or tenants, and (most important of all) they could be taken to court for breaking their obligations. In the course of a century or two, every town and city, every guild and university, acquired its own charter and its own corporate identity. The process reached its zenith in Russia, where the chartered and incorporated city-state of Novgorod had the legal status of a feudal overlord: the citizens swore allegiance to 'my lord Novgorod the Great'. To this day, in English law, one speaks (for instance) of 'the Corporation of the City of London', and when you have a grievance against the City for its collective misdeeds, you can sue the corporation instead of sending writs to the Lord Mayor in his unfortunate person.

All these kinds of corporations persist, of course, but they are overshadowed in the public mind by another kind of corporate body: the joint-stock company. Quite early on, men of business discovered that they could procure charters for particular enterprises, such as large-scale merchant shipping, or the building of dams and water works; and since the corporation had legal responsibility for its own debts and liabilities, a man could put money into such a business without fear of losing more than his initial investment. This idea of 'limited liability' made possible the entire process of capitalism and the whole system of the Industrial Revolution. At this moment, I am typing these words on a computer de-signed and marketed by one large corporation, assembled by another, with a microprocessor built by a third. Each of those firms uses equip-ment that cost many billions of dollars, beyond the ability of any one cap-italist to finance. When I am done, I shall offer this book for sale through still other corporations, and take advantage of their immense expertise and infrastructure to place my words before you, the reader. The joint-stock company is an excellent servant: it gives you and me the power to talk to one another. An excellent servant – but a terrible master.

For as Charles Williams' Taliessin warned us, the means tend to be-come autonomous. It is fashionable to inveigh against the wickedness and greed of corporations, and there is a good deal of truth in the accusa-tions. The greed of a joint-stock company is more or less built in. Busi-ness corporations are greedy for the same reason that cars all keep to one side of the road: there happens to be a law compelling them to do so. The laws concerning incorporated businesses impose a fiduciary duty on the directors of a firm – a duty to make the largest possible (and legal) profit for their shareholders. Greed as such is written into the charter of the in-corporated business. It is not written into the charter of a non-profit cor-poration, such as a charity or a university, or a governmental corporation, such as a town or a public utility. So far as it goes, this is a good thing, because it spells out clearly that the purpose of the business is to make money, and the purpose of the non-profit is something else entirely. But human beings are lazy and half-hearted, and tend to value security above liberty: liberty requires so much effort. They *allow* the means to become autonomous, because it takes hard work and intelligence to control them. Instead of ruling over their incorporated servants with a strict hand and a discerning eye, they go along to get along. The real sin of corporations is not greed but sloth.

A time comes when these slothful men awaken. Having built the corporations, invested in them, worked for them, paid taxes to them in labour and in cash, having done jobs they cared nothing about, having followed policies they hardly understood – having done all these things to evade personal responsibility, they find (to their inexplicable surprise) that they are no longer treated as responsible persons. The monster they built to serve them has become their master. And when the loss of freedom becomes too great – when the shoe pinches too hard to wear it any longer – then these slothful men awake, and find themselves in the belly of the dragon. Sauron gave Rings of Power to the Dwarves, promising them easy riches; in the end they got dragon-fire and slavery. We humans, without any rings of power, have taken a much shorter time to travel the same disastrous road.

Tolkien liked to say that Escape was one of the principal functions of fantasy – the escape of the prisoner, as he called it, contrasting it with the flight of the deserter. But there is also a fantasy that is the flight of the deserter – escapist in the bad sense and not the good. To slothful people, this escape takes the form of imagining that you can have a servant far greater than yourself, who nevertheless will never grow tired of serving you, and never make himself your master. This kind of escapism features strongly in the fantasies written by many of Tolkien's successors. From Anne McCaffrey on down through Disney and beyond, there has grown up a tradition of wise and powerful dragons who 'bond' with particular humans, lending them all their powers and becoming their willing slaves – though words like 'slave' are not generally used. It is the fantasy of Aladdin's lamp, without the moral lesson. The dragon, powerful and dangerous in himself, stops being the enemy of man and becomes, inexplicably, his willing subordinate. The genie was at least compelled by the magic of the lamp; the dragon, we are led to believe, goes into service merely for love of his human, that special and unique (and usually adolescent) snowflake. The dragon is transformed from a force of Nemesis into 'Your Reptile Pal Who's Fun To Be With'.

We may well imagine that in a world containing real live dragons, they would use such a device to deceive and subvert humans, as Sauron used the Rings to deceive and subvert the Dwarves. But the dragons themselves are not deceived. They know that these petty humans are not their masters but their pets; the relationship exists at the dragon's own pleasure, and ultimately for the dragon's own purposes. It would be a fine inversion of this post-Tolkien trope if a dragon's pet found out the real nature of the relationship, that 'Your Reptile Pal' was actually your lord and master, who kept you in a gilded cage but was bound to devour you in the end. No doubt such stories exist – any idea you can come up with in a moment's thought has already been tried a hundred times – but I do not know of any famous examples. The counter-trope has not yet become a trope in its own right. But the moral would be worth the tale. The people who give up their autonomy to businesses and bosses, parties and governments, and then complain because they are no longer autonomous, might at least be brought to see how foolish they are to complain. Their children (for any tale worth telling is worth telling to children) might even learn to spot the trap and refuse the bait.

The Tolkien Method, as I have called it, generates stories by resolving cruxes; and there is one crux concerning dragons that I have not yet mentioned, because Tolkien himself only indirectly addressed it. All that I have said about dragons, and the whole rich tradition that Tolkien drew on, comes out of the West, out of Greek and Norse folklore and kindred sources. There is, of course, another tradition about dragons, apparently at complete odds with the Western one. That is the Eastern tradition, the Chinese tradition chiefly, which depicts the dragon as a benevolent being, a keeper of order; indeed, one of these Eastern dragons is the personification of the Chinese Empire itself, and the alter ego of the Emperor. This is a fine test for the Method. If we can come up with some way of resolving *this* crux, marrying the Eastern with the Western dragon in a harmonious whole, then we may confidently suppose that the Method is strong enough to bear any narrative burden we could reasonably place upon it. I believe it can be done.

One of the most alien characteristics of Chinese civilization, to Western eyes, is the extreme subordination of the individual. The Western tradition is founded upon the value of the individual, and judges states and institutions by how well they serve the needs of men and women. The remark of Jesus, 'Remember that the Sabbath was made for man and not man for the Sabbath,' expresses the idea with his characteristic pith. In the Confucian world-view, such a saying would be almost meaningless. In that view, man is made for society, as surely as the organs of a man's body are made for the man. I have been told, in such a way as to believe it, that there used to be no native Chinese word for *individualism;* that where the concept was wanted, translators had to render the word into Chinese by a periphrasis, or else replace it with the Chinese word meaning *selfishness.* It might be excessive to say that in Confucianism mere selfhood is equated with selfishness, but it would be much nearer the truth than anything a Westerner would be inclined to accept.

Not that Tolkien would have subscribed to the merely libertarian idea of the individual as ultimate sovereign. He was a Catholic, a devout and learned one, and his thoughts were predicated upon Catholic theology to a remarkable degree. To such a man, the ultimate sovereign, and the primary source of reality, is of course God; but Man has a reality that flows directly from God, and everything between them is only a means to an end. Society, the state, the Church, and (as Jesus said) the Law and the Sabbath, are all made for man; more precisely, they are made to help put man in the right relation with God. God is the lodestone, man is the iron, and if each atom of iron is aligned correctly with the lodestone, the whole mass will be magnetized. That, approximately, is the Catholic ideal of society. It is for this reason that the Church is officially indifferent to political systems. A monarchy, an aristocracy, a democracy, or even a dictatorship may, from the Catholic point of view, be the system of government most appropriate for a particular people in particular conditions. The whole question is whether the structure of society allows men and women to be in the correct relationship with God.

The nearest Confucian analogue to this idea, perhaps, is what is called 'the Mandate of Heaven'. It is taken for granted that society will take a monarchical form, and an absolute monarchy at that; the idea of a law which is above kings and emperors never really took hold in Chinese jurisprudence. But it is possible for an emperor to lose the Mandate of Heaven, if he is no longer able to keep harmony and order among his subjects; and then he may be legitimately overthrown. But this is not thought of as being done in the interest of the subjects; primarily it is done in the interest of the empire itself. The larger unit takes precedence over the smaller. The empire is not a means to keep the people in a right relationship with Heaven; the empire is itself in a right relationship with Heaven, or else the Mandate of Heaven is withdrawn. It is the job of the people to put themselves in a right relationship with the Imperial hierarchy. The Western idea of charters and corporations could not well have arisen in a Confucian society: for a charter conferred a legal right that even a king was bound to respect, whereas every right conferred by a Chinese emperor may be revoked at the emperor's pleasure. It is, in a less naked and more philosophical form, the idea of totalitarianism: 'All within the State, nothing outside the State, nothing against the State.' As we have seen in the last century, what totalitarian régimes do best is produce mountains of corpses. We should therefore expect to find such mountains in Chinese history; and we will not be mistaken. The Taiping Rebellion, for instance, produced a greater death-toll than any conflict in Western history before the First World War.

What, then, do we make of the wise and benevolent Eastern dragon? I have suggested that when the Western dragon pretends to become the servant of a particular human, the dragon is not deceived, and the human is kept as a pet. It is not hard to imagine that a dragon could find it more profitable to pose as the protector of humans, to collect them and employ their labour for its own enrichment: in fact, to *domesticate* them, instead of treating them as prey. On this assumption, the fantasy equivalent of the Chinese Empire would be a Draconic Empire, in which the ruling caste of dragons (and the great Imperial Dragon himself) keep the human population as cattle – a gigantic ranch, and potentially a hugely profitable one. There are instances in human history of subjugated nations being systematically milked in this way – Egypt under the Ptolemies, for instance. An empire-building dragon could, over the course of centuries, accumulate fantastic profits for itself, without any of the risks involved in killing people and taking away their treasure. If the dragon was sufficiently adept at propaganda, no doubt it could convince its milch cows that the whole arrangement was part of the natural order.

We will not find such an imperial dragon in Tolkien; but we will find Sauron, in his guise as 'Lord of Gifts' and ruler of Middle-earth. Glaurung, in some of the *Silmarillion* texts, appears as a kind of warlord in Morgoth's service, ruling over his own fief and his own Orcish armies from the ruins of Nargothrond. Sauron does the same on a far larger scale, and with better servants than Orcs. The tendency of every totalitarian state is to try to enlarge itself; there have never been two totalitarianisms that got along easily together – *serpens nisi serpentem comederit*. One dragon always tends to eat another. The ultimate fantasy of dragonkind is of the single Great Dragon that encompasses the whole world, hoards it, and ultimately devours it.

This is an image that recurs in mythology all over the world; it is most often depicted as a giant serpent swallowing its own tail – feeding on itself because nothing else is left to sate its hunger. The Greeks called it Ouroboros; the Norse called it Jörmungandr, or Midgarðsormr, the Middle-earth Serpent. The Ouroboros motif occurs in art and folklore all over the world – particularly in India, Egypt, and Mesoamerica, besides the places just mentioned. It is a recurrent theme in painting and sculpture, and also in jewellery; and it should come as no surprise (given the shape of a serpent biting its own tail) that it is often fashioned into a ring. Magical powers have been attributed to such rings.

In a highly stylized and symbolic way, the Ouroboros, the World Serpent, of Tolkien's Middle-earth is the One Ring itself. It embodies Sauron's ultimate urge to power, which encompasses and surpasses all the lesser lusts of the dragons and their surrogates. It is Sauron's own dominating will, which he made separate from himself out of necessity: anything you send forth to rule over others, to that extent, becomes separate from yourself. A master of slaves becomes dependent on his slaves, and on the obedience and fear he has put into their minds. Sauron became so dependent on his Ring that, though naturally immortal, he could not survive its destruction. In folklore, in pagan tradition, the World Serpent is the symbol of the world. In Tolkien, the One Ring becomes the symbol of Sauron's desire: a world utterly ruled by his will, completely contained within his swollen self, where nothing would ever happen again except the constant self-devouring of Sauron exerting power over his own extended body – Middle-earth itself. No dragon could want for more.

MOORCOCK, SARUMAN,
AND THE DRAGON'S TAIL

T
he journalist and historian Paul Johnson has divided all serious writers and critics into two camps, 'intellectuals' and 'men of letters'. Intellectuals are those who, like Shelley, conceive themselves to be 'the unacknowledged legislators of the world'; they are the Utopians, the revolutionists, the Angry Young Men; they involve themselves in politics, usually radical, readily form claques, and have a disturbing tendency to write manifestos. Men of letters (the term dates back to less literal-minded times, when 'men' could be understood to refer to both sexes) just read things, and write things, and write about what they read. They do not even have a strong tendency to read about what they write: the Platonically ideal man of letters is too comfortable in his ivory tower to care much about reviews and Press clippings. Karl Marx could well stand for the purest form of intellectual, and Emily Dickinson, if you will pardon the Irish bull, was a perfect man of letters.

Of course these extremes are only the endpoints of a continuous line, but most authors show a definite tendency to drift towards one end or the other. Tolstoy was an intellectual, and developed the points of that breed, so to speak, more and more strongly as he grew older, until he gave up imaginative writing altogether in favour of his own weird form of political messianism. Shakespeare was a man of letters, so very much so that it is still hotly disputed what his political opinions were, or whether he ever troubled to form any. Intellectuals have often been quick to dismiss men of letters as reactionary toadies or commercial hacks, and in fact Tolstoy attacked Shakespeare as both in his pamphlet, *Shakespeare and the Drama*. But for all the fame of both the attacker and the target, that pamphlet would be forgotten today, had it not been preserved by George Orwell's much more famous rebuttal, 'Lear, Tolstoy, and the Fool'. On the whole Orwell was an intellectual, but he had a strong streak of the man of letters in him, and his sympathies were very much with Shakespeare.

In our own time, Michael Moorcock could well be described as an intellectual who sometimes masquerades as a man of letters. In *The Way the Future Was,* Frederik Pohl says that if the Futurians had conquered all of science-fiction fandom, the mere world would have been an anticlimax; and the same quality is distinctly present in Moorcock's characteristic literary polemics. He takes literature as his battleground, but his weapons and his enmities are drawn from an almost purely political ideology. He seems very much concerned that Utopian writers shall write about the *correct* kind of Utopia, and his fury with dissenters knows no bounds. J. R. R. Tolkien, on the other hand, was so very much a man of letters that he did not even attempt to publish any of his fiction until a reader at Allen and Unwin chanced to hear of *The Hobbit* and pried the typescript out of his hands. And while Tolkien seems not to have read Moorcock any more than Shakespeare could have read Tolstoy, the same kind of bitter one-way enmity has grown between them.

I have before me an essay of Moorcock's, called 'Wit and Humour in Fantasy', first published in 1979. It is ostensibly an argument for the natural and necessary alliance between humour and fantasy (something nobody ever remarked upon before Moorcock); but he makes his argument very badly, partly because it is poppycock, but chiefly because his real purpose is to attack his arch-enemy, Tolkien. In consequence it makes for interesting reading, and I would nominate it for a place of honour beside *Shakespeare and the Drama* in the canon of foolish diatribes.

Like Tolstoy's, Moorcock's essay is not easy to find in print, and so, like Orwell, I shall begin with a summary. He starts off with a quotation from Scott's *Peverile of the Peak,* saying that Scott's wit redeemed his work and makes it readable today, 'though', says Moorcock, 'he spread it as thinly as he spread the rest of his talents'. Then he proceeds directly to his thesis, which is happily brief and quotable:

> Fantastic fiction is happily very rich in comedy, from Thomas Love Peacock to Mervyn Peake. Comedy demands paradox – the juxtaposition of disparate images and elements – just as fantasy does. The square peg was never more delightful than when trying to fit itself into the round hole of a de Camp and Pratt fantasy. Comedy – like fantasy – is often at its best when making the greatest possible exaggerations – whereas tragedy usually becomes bathetic when it exaggerates.

As examples of successful comedy in fantasy he offers *A Connecticut Yankee in King Arthur's Court,* Cabell's *Biography of the Life of Manuel,* Fritz Leiber's Fafhrd stories, even *Howard the Duck*; but he reserves his highest accolades for Mervyn Peake's series, which he (along with nearly everyone else) incorrectly calls 'the *Gormenghast* trilogy'. I shall return to this later.

Throughout the essay, Moorcock mingles passages of eminent good sense with pronunciamentos so peculiar that they simply leave one shaking one's head. He finds humour in the oddest places, and in the oddest proportions, too. Moorcock is not himself known as a humorous writer, and that, coupled with the examples he offers as masterworks of wit, makes him look rather like a man trying to sing in the opera, who, while perfectly versed in music theory, happens to be completely tone-deaf. But let us be fair, and begin with the eminent good sense. Some representative samples:

> What gives Twain's romance a power which its imitators have in the main lacked is the undercurrent of pathos and tragedy running through the whole story.

The optimist and the pessimist constantly war within the writer of fiction as he gives shape to his chosen subject matter. But it should be the subject matter, not the author's wishes, which ultimately speaks for itself. If the author forces the material one way or another to achieve a happy or an unhappy ending and thus denies the implications of what he has written he is betraying both the reader and himself.

Horace Walpole said that life was a comedy to those that think, a tragedy to those that feel. Since it is fair to guess that the majority of us both think and feel it is fair to expect fiction which appeals to both our thoughts and our emotions.

But a writer must entertain before he has any right to try instruction. . . . An artist cannot be much of a politician, unless it is during his time off.

To be a victim of one's own messianism is terrible – to become the victim of someone else's is even worse.

All good sound advice; and even if a novice writer is so great a blockhead that he cannot benefit from any of it, at least it will do him no harm. Moorcock himself would do well to be reminded at times of the last sentence quoted above.

But let us take a closer look at what Moorcock takes for wit and humour. He speaks highly of Leiber's use of humour:

To off-set the grandiose, the pompous elements in fantasy, the writer like Fritz Leiber will introduce comedy to 'humanise' the characters and make the reader much more concerned in their fate. . . .

I have only a slight acquaintance with Leiber's work, but those who know him better offer a rather different verdict. Here is Ursula K.

LeGuin, a critic of honest genius, in the endlessly quotable 'From Elfland to Poughkeepsie':

> Fritz Leiber and Roger Zelazny have both written in the comic-heroic vein, but their technique is different: they alternate the two styles. When humor is intended the characters talk colloquial American English, or even slang, and at earnest moments they revert to old formal usages. Readers indifferent to language do not mind this, but for others the strain is too great. I am one of these latter. I am jerked back and forth between Elfland and Poughkeepsie; the characters lose coherence in my mind, and I lose confidence in them.

It strikes me that this points up the greatest weakness in Moorcock's argument. Fantasy and comedy may both take colour from exaggeration, but it is done for different purposes and in different directions. Actually exaggeration is nothing like so great an element in fantasy as Moorcock makes out. The juxtaposition of disparate elements, as he puts it, is often most effective when kept simple. The dragon, putting 'hot fire into the belly of the cold worm' as Tolkien said, is a much more successful juxtaposition than the cockatrice, the griffin, or the chimaera; indeed, the last of these has become a byword for a hybrid too bizarre to be viable. The more animals you throw into the genetic blender, the less convincing the result tends to be. A lion's head, a goat's body, a serpent's tail, and dragon-fire in the lungs: the combination is too obviously arbitrary. If you exaggerate the strangeness of comedy, progressing by degrees from a plausible beginning, you may produce a brilliant series of toppers; if you exaggerate the strangeness of fantasy, you will only strain your audience's credulity and break the suspension of disbelief. This introduces a tension between the two literary effects, the comical and the fantastic, that greatly increases the difficulty of combining them well.

All this is mixed in with a rather different line of argument, a direct and rather bitter polemic directed against Moorcock's most successful competitors, Tolkien and Heinlein. One almost feels that he champions the cause of humour specifically so that he can do dirt on writers he dislikes, and in fact he comes near to admitting as much himself:

> While I admire the work of James Branch Cabell, I find his ironies too relentless. He cheats in order to show everything as an example of mere human folly. In contrast to Twain, he uses his talents almost always to avoid pain, though he uses them very cleverly. . . . Cabell's kind of fiction may well act as a fine antidote to Tolkien's, but neither is very satisfying to the demanding reader in the long run.

For 'the demanding reader', read Moorcock himself. It is a common rhetorical trick designed to bamboozle the inexperienced. 'If you were really a sophisticated reader,' he implies, 'you would know better than to read that *Lord of the Rings* rubbish.' The use of the word 'antidote', as if Tolkien were a poison, is a sly rhetorical touch. Cabell isn't really good for you, you see, but at least he'll cure you of Tolkien. The enemy of my enemy is my friend.

But here, scarcely three pages into the essay, is the nub of his case against Tolkien:

> It seems always to have been true that the more grandiose, the more portentous, the less concise, the less truthful, the more humourless a writer is, the more successful he is; at least in immediate terms.

Let us note in passing that this seems *not* always, or indeed ever, to have been true. *Huckleberry Finn, Tom Jones, The Pickwick Papers, Alice's Adventures in Wonderland,* and *Catch-22,* were each of them an immediate commercial success as well as an enduring critical success; and none of them can be called grandiose, or portentous, or mendacious, or (least of all) humourless. *Tristram Shandy* was a tissue of *longueurs,* I will grant, but it lacked the other four of Moorcock's sneering prerequisites for commercial success. But to continue:

I think my own dislike of J. R. R. Tolkien lies primarily in the fact that in all those hundreds of pages, full of high ideals, sinister evil and noble deeds, there is scarcely a hint of irony anywhere. Its tone is one of relentless nursery room sobriety. 'Once upon a time,' began nanny gravely, for telling stories was a series [*sic*] matter, 'there were a lot of furry little people who lived happily in the most beautiful, gentlest countryside you could possibly imagine, and then one day they learned that Wicked Outsiders were threatening this peace. . . .'

Now, this is almost as gross a misrepresentation of *The Lord of the Rings* as Tolstoy's account of one of King Lear's speeches: 'Again begin Lear's awful ravings, at which one feels ashamed, as at unsuccessful jokes.' One can hardly feel that either Tolstoy or Moorcock is even trying to be honest. Tolstoy is determined that people shall not enjoy Shakespeare, and Moorcock is determined that they shall not enjoy Tolkien, and any stick will do to beat a dog. Shall we catalogue the smears, innuendoes, and outright lies in that passage?

To begin with, 'relentless sobriety' is hardly a quality most people would ascribe to the nursery, but let that pass. The image of a nanny telling portentous stories (as if they were ghost stories) to her charges is a deliberate falsification of what Tolkien set out to do. He sometimes took that tone in *The Hobbit*, a thing he came to regret bitterly, but *The Lord of the Rings* was written consciously and skilfully for an adult audience. Except for one or two minor stumbles in the opening chapters, there is no talking-down in it anywhere.

The snide pun about 'series matter' is magnificently cheeky, coming from a man whose principal fantasy works, to the tune of some fifteen volumes, are rolled up into the gigantic *Eternal Champion* series; furthermore, it is wide of the mark, for *The Lord of the Rings,* long though it may be, is not a series except for convenience of binding. This is on a par with Virginia Woolf's famous sneer about 'four-volume novels', except that Woolf at least was not guilty of the alleged sin she was denouncing. Moorcock is merely hypocritical.

The Shire may be 'the gentlest countryside you could imagine', but so is the English countryside on which it was faithfully based. Actually all of Tolkien's settings are beautiful, when not blasted and ruined by Orcs, dragons, or Dark Lords; indeed, his fame as a literary stylist rests largely upon his skill at describing the beauty of nature. In this he is a true heir of the Romantic poets, and most particularly of Wordsworth, who was also bitterly castigated by many of the other Romantics because he rejected their radical politics. I cannot remember a vivid description of scenery anywhere in Moorcock, and he gives rather the impression of piquing himself on his indifference to such trivialities. But in fact a love of nature is not a mark of childishness, and it is disingenuous of him to imply that it is.

'One day they learned that Wicked Outsiders were threatening this peace.' As it happens, this, more than anything else in the opening of *The Lord of the Rings,* shows Tolkien's masterly handling of irony. That the Shire is threatened by sinister external forces is obvious almost from the start. Sam Gamgee's cousin Hal has seen giants on the borders, and the dwarves who pass through the Shire speak of Orcs, trolls, and the growing shadow of Mordor; but the Hobbits, so smugly insular that their very maps show only white space beyond the bounds of the Shire, refuse to believe any of these stories. Ted Sandyman dismisses Sam's account with sneers and sophistry, and shows himself to be both a typical Hobbit (though more mechanically inclined than most) and a thoroughly disagreeable character. It is the same irony that Douglas Adams made explicit with his Ravenous Bugblatter Beast of Traal, which is so stupid that it thinks it can't see you if you can't see it, and is completely foiled if you wrap a towel round your head. The Hobbits, so to speak, have had towels wrapped round their heads for generations, and it works for them no better than one would expect. The moment the Rangers withdraw their protection, ruffians and half-Orcs descend upon the Shire, and Saruman comes to turn it into a faithful copy of the polluted desert of Mordor. This is a very subtle and well-informed bit of satire, directed squarely against

Tolkien's fellow Englishmen, who had similar delusions of invulnerabil-
ity.

Perhaps Moorcock cannot perceive this irony, in which case I could
only wonder that he thinks himself fit to criticize *any* work of serious
literature. I perceived it myself when I was twelve, and had lived a life
almost as sheltered as a Hobbit's. I think it more likely that he is merely
being disingenuous. In fact, I am certain of it, for he also has this to say:

> There are, of course, some whimsical jokes in Tolkien, some
> 'universal ironies', but these only serve to exaggerate the pau-
> city of genuine imaginative invention.

Let me pause again to admire the audacity of this statement. If there
is one thing Tolkien is famous for, it is the abounding fertility of his imaginative invention. Even most critics who dislike *The Lord of the Rings*
pay grudging tribute to the size, scope, and sheer technical difficulty of
Tolkien's elaborate invention of Middle-earth.

> The jokes are not there to point to the truth, but to reject it. The
> collapse down the centuries of the great myths into nursery
> tales is mirrored in recent fiction. We have gone from hobbits,
> to seagulls, to rabbits and a whole host of other assorted talking
> vermin in a few short years. . . .

People were telling stories about talking animals thousands of years
ago; Aesop specialized in it; the tradition has continued without inter-
ruption from that day to this. *Jonathan Livingston Seagull* bears no resemblance to anything by Tolkien, and *Watership Down* is if anything
elevated from a 'talking vermin' story by the epic tone it copies from
Tolkien. It is a gross and obvious lie to blame Tolkien for the existence
of talking-animal stories, but again, any stick will do to beat that dog.
Now, incidentally, we see why Moorcock made the error of calling Hobbits 'furry'. They are nothing of the kind; they do not have more body hair
than humans, merely a different distribution. But by implying that they

are some kind of lower animal instead of, as Tolkien explicitly described them, a divergent branch of the human race, he makes the link to 'talking vermin' superficially plausible.

He raises against Tolkien (and even more specifically against Heinlein) the old, threadbare charge of 'escapism':

> The laboured irony, as it were, of the pulp hero or heroine, this deadly levity in the fact of genuine experience, which serves not to point up the dramatic effect of the narrative, but to reduce it – and to make the experience described comfortably 'unreal' – is the trick of the truly escapist author who pretends to be writing about fundamental truths and is in fact telling fundamental lies.

There, I think, is where the shoe pinches. Let us look at some of the 'fundamental lies' Tolkien offers us:

Power is addictive.

The habitual exercise of power corrodes the will and blunts the moral sense.

There is evil in the world that we cannot hope to overcome, but it will never be overcome unless we do what we can to resist it.

By conquering nature, we dehumanize ourselves, but by appreciating nature and preserving it, we supply a deep spiritual need.

Good cannot be achieved by evil means. Moreover, evil itself cannot achieve the particular ends it desires by evil means: 'Oft evil will shall evil mar.'

There is no good excuse for cooperating with a tyrant. If you think he will spare you because of it, you are fooling yourself.

It is better to resist evil, even if it means war, than submit peacefully to be enslaved and slaughtered.

The desire for immortality is a cheat, for no matter how much power you have, you will never have power over death.

If we oppose evil to the limit of our strength, though that in itself is inadequate, there is a Providence that can make our victory possible.

I think it is this last point above all that offends Moorcock. He is bitterly hostile to religion, and to Christianity in particular, and his own fiction does not suggest that he has a well-developed sense of ethics. The great struggle in the Elric books is not between Good and Evil, nor even between better and worse impulses in the human mind, but between Law and Chaos, either of which can be served just as well by evil means as by good. Actually it is a false dichotomy, as Fabio P. Barbieri has pointed out. Chaos can only occur in a context of order, and order, by the laws of thermodynamics, inevitably decays into chaos. The alternative to an ordered society is not a state of complete anarchy, but death; and everything that exists, however disorderly it may appear, is strictly subject to the laws that make its existence possible. As William Blake said, 'Reason is the circumference of energy': they require each other, like the poles of a magnet. But since neither law nor chaos can exist alone, there can be no final victory or defeat in any war between them. The combatants can go on fighting for ever, or at least until they grow tired and discover that the whole donnybrook was fundamentally silly.

Elric makes a pact with Arioch, a Lord of Chaos, who gives him the sword Stormbringer. Stormbringer gives its wielder great power, but also turns him, in effect, into a vampire, who must slay other living souls merely to stay alive. Nowhere in the Elric books is there much indication that Moorcock's hero regrets his pact, or feels that his victims have any worth comparable to his own. In the end he builds up an army of barbarians, returns to Melniboné, kills the cousin who usurped his throne, destroys the entire city, and then betrays his allies to destruction themselves. From all this slaughter and betrayal he walks away more or less smiling, if the desperately melancholy Elric can ever be said to smile. It is a celebration of heroic nihilism so blatant that even Nietzsche might have averted his eyes in shame. All this is worlds away from the strict Judaeo-Christian ethics and Catholic sense of grace that permeate Tolkien's work. Moorcock is not the only critic to have scented the presence of grace and reacted like Gollum to *lembas:* 'Leaves out of the elf-country, gah! Dust and ashes, we can't eat that.' It is significant that Moorcock is a strong admirer of Philip Pullman, whose entire oeuvre is essentially an attack on a Gnosticized straw-man version of Christianity.

Orwell observed that of all Shakespeare's plays, Tolstoy chose to attack *King Lear*; and he attributed this to Tolstoy's recognition, perhaps subconscious, of an unflattering resemblance between Lear and himself. Both men gave up their lands and their worldly power, and their families and flatterers turned against them for it. Renunciation brought neither man the happiness he expected, but a depth of misery founded upon his own ignorance of human nature. Moorcock's attack on Tolkien is so general, and he so carefully refuses to *name* the 'fundamental lies' and 'whimsical jokes' of which he accuses him, that it is not so easy to tell if a particular character affected him in this way. But one could make a case for it. I can see points of resemblance, just as unflattering, between Moorcock and Saruman the White.

As Tom Shippey observes in *Tolkien: Author of the Century*, Saruman is by far the most modern character in Middle-earth. His style varies between the pompous circumlocution of a Parliamentary white paper and the cant of a left-wing ideologue. Like Moorcock's most characteristic heroes, he has little use for outworn Scholastic categories like Good and Evil; he is a 'realist', full of geopolitical calculations and *raisons d'état*. Here he is as reported by Gandalf at the Council of Elrond, striking his most characteristic note:

> 'A new Power is rising. Against it the old allies and policies will avail us not at all. There is no hope left in Elves or dying Nú-menor. This then is the one choice before you, before us. We may join with that Power. It would be wise, Gandalf. There is hope that way. Its victory is at hand; and there will be a rich reward for those that aided it. As the Power grows, its proved friends will also grow; and the Wise, such as you and I, may with patience come at last to direct its courses, to control it. We can bide our time, we can keep our thoughts in our hearts,

deploring maybe evils done by the way, but approving the high and ultimate purpose: Knowledge, Rule, Order; all the things that we have so far striven in vain to accomplish, hindered rather than helped by our weak or idle friends. There need not be, there would not be, any real change in our designs, only in our means.'

So spoke Laval and Quisling and Seyss-Inquart, in the very days when Tolkien was writing that bitter parody of their words and attitudes. If Moorcock cannot perceive the irony in Saruman's speech, then I account him no judge. But if he can, it must wound him bitterly, for Moorcock himself has a tendency to talk that way, and his so-called heroes, Elric most notably, live on a moral plane from which they could only look up at Saruman as an impossible idealist. Tolkien's villains are more heroic than Moorcock's heroes, and the reading public knows it: a standing rebuke that Moorcock apparently cannot bear.

But to return to this matter of Moorcock's own lack of humour. His highest praise is for Mervyn Peake, and indeed the two books set in Gormenghast are masterpieces of their kind. There is even a kind of cult of Peake, founded perhaps by Moorcock and his fellow-travellers, which sets him up in opposition to Tolkien and then proclaims him to be the greater of the two. He is the British Left's answer to Tolkien, rather as the Monkees were America's answer to the Beatles; and while Peake is a far greater artist than the Monkees, he is no more adequate to bear the burden of such a comparison than they were.

Here (and I apologize for quoting at such length) is what Moorcock calls 'a short passage from the under-rated third volume, *Titus Alone*', and offers as a sublime example of Peake's uproarious humour:

> The Magistrate leaned forward on his elbows and rested his long, bony chin upon the knuckles of his interlocked fingers.
>
> 'This is the fourth time that I have had you before me at the bar, and as far as I can judge, the whole thing has been a waste of time to the Court and nothing but a nuisance to myself. Your

answers, when they have been forthcoming, have been either idiotic, nebulous, or fantastic. This cannot be allowed to go on. Your youth is no excuse. Do you like stamps?'

'Stamps, your Worship?'

'Do you collect them?'

'No.'

'A pity. I have a rare collection rotting daily. Now listen to me. You have already spent a week in prison – but it is not your vagrancy that troubles me. That is straightforward, though culpable. It is that you are rootless and obtuse. It seems you have some knowledge hidden from us. Your ways are curious, your terms are meaningless. I will ask you once again. What is this Gormenghast? What does it mean?'

Titus turned his face to the Bench. If ever there was a man to be trusted, his Worship was that man.

Ancient, wrinkled, like a tortoise, but with eyes as candid as grey glass.

But Titus made no answer, only brushing his forehead with the sleeve of his coat.

'Have you heard his Worship's question?' said a voice at his side. It was Mr Drugg.

'I do not know,' said Titus, 'what is meant by such a question. You might just as well ask me what is this hand of mine? What does it mean?' And he raised it in the air with the fingers spread out like a starfish. 'Or what is this leg?' And he stood on one foot in the box and shook the other as though it were loose. 'Forgive me, your Worship, I cannot understand.'

'It is a *place,* your Worship,' said the Clerk of the Court. 'The prisoner has insisted that it is a *place.*'

'Yes, yes,' said the Magistrate. 'But where is it? Is it north, south, east, or west, young man? Help *me* to help *you.* I take it you do not want to spend the rest of your life sleeping on the roofs of foreign towns. What is it boy? What is the matter with you?'

A ray of light slid through a high window of the Courtroom and hit the back of Mr Drugg's short neck as though it were revealing something of mystical significance. Mr Drugg drew back his head and the light moved forward and settled on his ear. Titus watched it as he spoke.

'I would tell you if I could, sir,' he said. 'I only know that I have lost my way. It is not that I want to return to my home – I do not; it is that even if I wished to do so I could not. It is not that I have travelled very far; it is that I have lost my bearings, sir.'

'Did you run away, young man?'

'I rode away,' said Titus.

'From ... Gormenghast?'

'Yes, your Worship.'

'Leaving your mother ... ?'

'Yes.'

'And your father ... ?'

'No, not my father ...'

'Ah ... is he dead, my boy?'

'Yes, your Worship. He was eaten by owls.'

The Magistrate raised an eyebrow and began to write upon a piece of paper.

Now, I have tried that passage upon various persons of my acquaintance, including some of the most keenly humorous that I know, and people who enjoy Mervyn Peake, too; and none of them could find anything so very funny in it. At most they get a dry little chuckle out of the bit about the stamps, and another, perhaps, about the light on Mr. Drugg's ear; and a slight smile of recognition at the mention of the owls. Humour is notoriously a subjective thing, but there is, so to speak, a main current, and this is nowhere near it. I may add on my own showing that I do not find *Titus Alone* underrated at all; I was physically unable to finish it. It is a disconnected string of rather dreary episodes, haunted by the ghost of Peake's declining wit, for he was terminally ill when he wrote it. No doubt the Peake who wrote *Titus Groan* could have made this scene sprightly and funny and poignant. In the hands of his older and wearier self, it just lies there, glinting dully. I had no trouble finishing either *Titus Groan* or *Gormenghast,* though taken together they are nearly as long as *The Lord of the Rings;* but the accumulation of tedious inconsequentialities, like dead leaves in a rain-gutter, in *Titus Alone* put me to sleep before I could finish a book of little more than two hundred pages.

Here, on the other hand, is an extract from a different work, which I find to contain more laughs per paragraph than the excerpt above has in its entire length:

> But more news came in next day. The dragon, it appeared, was exceptionally large and ferocious. He was doing terrible damage.
>
> 'What about the King's knights?' people began to say.
>
> Others had already asked the same question. Indeed, messengers were now reaching the King from the villages most affected by Chrysophylax, and they said to him as loudly and as often as they dared: 'Lord, what of your knights?'
>
> But the knights did nothing; their knowledge of the dragon was still quite unofficial. So the King brought the matter to their notice, fully and formally, asking for necessary action at their early convenience. He was greatly displeased when he found that their convenience would not be early at all, and was indeed daily postponed.
>
> Yet the excuses of the knights were undoubtedly sound. First of all, the Royal Cook had already made the Dragon's Tail for that Christmas, being a man who believed in getting things done in good time. It would not do at all to offend him by bringing in a real tail at the last minute. He was a very valuable servant.
>
> 'Never mind the Tail! Cut his head off and put an end to him!' cried the messengers from the villages most nearly affected.

But Christmas had arrived, and most unfortunately a grand tournament had been arranged for St. John's Day: knights of many realms had been invited and were coming to compete for a valuable prize. It was obviously unreasonable to spoil the chances of the Midland Knights by sending their best men off on a dragon-hunt before the tournament was over.

After that came the New Year Holiday.

But each night the dragon had moved; and each move had brought him nearer to Ham. On the night of New Year's Day people could see a blaze in the distance. The dragon had settled in a wood about ten miles away, and it was burning merrily. He was a hot dragon when he felt in the mood.

I could ask you to think it a happy coincidence that this happens to be from *Farmer Giles of Ham,* by none other than J. R. R. Tolkien, but of course it is no coincidence at all. Perhaps you do not find it any funnier than Moorcock's pet passage from Peake; but it is said that the Lovelace Society at Worcester College was convulsed with laughter when Tolkien read it aloud for them. At any rate it shows that the alleged lack of humour in *The Lord of the Rings* did not result from any incapacity on Tolkien's part. You might suppose that Moorcock would think better of it than of Tolkien's major works; but I doubt he has ever read it, for the stink of the author's name still clings to it. 'Leaves out of the elf-country, gah!' Besides, as I have said, I very much doubt whether Moorcock's real objection to Tolkien has anything to do with humour at all. He just hates him so bitterly that he must drag him in by the heels, and spoil an otherwise interesting essay with a mean-spirited and irrelevant attack.

This is how Orwell ends his essay on Tolstoy and Shakespeare:

> Tolstoy was perhaps the most admired literary man of his age, and he was certainly not its least able pamphleteer. He turned all his powers of denunciation against Shakespeare, like all the guns of a battleship roaring simultaneously. And with what result? Forty years later Shakespeare is still there completely un-

affected, and of the attempt to demolish him nothing remains except the yellowing pages of a pamphlet which hardly anyone has read, and which would be forgotten altogether if Tolstoy had not also been the author of *War and Peace* and *Anna Karenina*.

Mutatis mutandis, I could say the same. Moorcock is one of the most prestigious authors and critics of our age, and certainly not its least able essayist. He has repeatedly turned all his powers of denunciation against Tolkien, like all the guns of a battleship roaring simultaneously. And with what result? Thirty years later Tolkien is still there completely unaffected, and of the attempt to demolish him nothing remains except the yellowing pages of an essay which hardly anyone has read, and which would be forgotten altogether if Moorcock were not still alive among us, beating forlornly at the same hollow drum. Like Nietzsche's battle against God, Moorcock's battle against Tolkien will die with him. There will always be others to take up their own personal quarrels on their own personal grounds; but theirs is a war that can never be won.

THE ABYSS AND THE CRITICS
(A review of *The Children of Húrin*)

As Tom Shippey rightly points out, Tolkien has not been well served by his critics. On the one hand you have the *literati*, the self-appointed Guardians of the Tradition, who have never overcome their collective indignation at the success of *The Lord of the Rings*, but somehow have never quite died of collective apoplexy either. This contingent is ably represented, this time out, by Marta Salij of the *Detroit Free Press* and Tom Deveson of the *Times*. I shall come back to Ms. Salij's brand of incomprehension later, but here is a fair sample of Mr. Deveson's hard work in establishing his credentials as one of those who just don't get it:

> Turin is captivated by 'the Sindarin tongue', 'older, and ... rich-
> er in beautiful words'. Tolkien endorses this equation of archa-
> ism with beauty, but doesn't show why it is more desirable to
> write 'dwelt' than 'lived', to describe a sword that 'would cleave
> all earth-dolven iron' or to have people say, 'Await me here until
> haply I return.'

After reading that, I spent half an hour combing through *The Children of Húrin* line by line, looking for the sentence that Mr. Deveson found so needless and offensive. It is dialogue, of course, Morwen's last words to her daughter Niënor before setting out to find her son. That is a perilous quest, and indeed a hopeless one, as Thingol and Melian, her hosts and protectors, have warned her. But as we so often do, she makes a decision in a moment of high emotion and then sticks to it out of stubborn pride, letting no counsel sway her.

Tolkien knew better than any author of his time the uses of archaism, and the tricks and techniques of inserting them successfully into more or less modern English. *Haply* is a good deal more archaic than most of the vocabulary in *Children,* though not too antique for the style. Yet Tolkien produced many of his best effects by coupling archaic syntax with deliberately ordinary vocabulary. Why did he reach for a half-forgotten word in this case? The best answer is the one he gave to Hugh Brogan:

> Real archaic English is far more *terse* than modern; also many of the things said could not be said in our slack and often frivolous idiom.

I have, as it happens, some experience of précis work, and of editing texts to various lengths; I know how sloppy most modern writers are. Had I the time to dehydrate all the English prose that is published each day, I could liberate enough water to run Niagara Falls out of business. The sentence Mr. Deveson objects to is as dry as ship's biscuit. If you take it apart, and put it back together in purely modern English, it means: 'Wait for me here until I come back – if that ever happens.' That takes twelve words to Tolkien's seven. Morwen's almost parenthetical use of *haply* expresses all the fatality of her decision and the fatalism of her outlook, and does it in a way that no other single English word can match. She is fey, desperate, and almost hopeless, and Tolkien shows us the extremity of her plight without a word of narrative. That, Mr. Deveson, is why *haply* is desirable.

On the other hand we have the gushing reviews of the fans, the completists who would have it that every word to drop from the master's pen must be equally admired. It takes a very great author indeed to survive the sycophancy of his friends. Tolkien was not quite up to the task; but then, neither was Shakespeare. Tolkien wrote his full share of tosh and drivel; some of the worst can be found in the two volumes of *The Book of Lost Tales,* especially the verses, which after all he wrote in his early twenties. We must all learn our craft somewhere. Few have mastered it as thoroughly as Tolkien, or with such herculean effort: he did not persevere in vain. But then few of us are so unfortunate as to have our early efforts published and preserved. There are fans, I suppose, who claim that the *Lost Tales* are great work in themselves, just as there have been idolaters of Shakespeare who called *Titus Andronicus* a classic.

When *The Silmarillion* came out, thousands of readers tried hard to like it, failed, and refused to confess their failure. When the *Lost Tales* came out, thousands who had enjoyed *The Silmarillion* repeated the process. Lately the buzz has been that *Children* is a return to the novelistic style of *The Lord of the Rings,* more accessible than *The Silmarillion.* We have been told so by a formidable array of Tolkienists, Tolkienians, Tolkienologists, Tolkienosophers, Tolkienographers, and Tolkienicians, most of whom had never seen the book themselves when they issued these favourable pronunciamentos. Now I am not a Tolkienist, a Tolkienian, a Tolkienologist, a Tolkienosopher, a Tolkienographer, or a Tolkienician, but I have at least read the book; and in my considered opinion, we have been told a whopper. This new volume is as accessible as *The Silmarillion* itself, and no more, or very little; and for very much the same reasons.

The Children of Húrin could have been as accessible as anything Tolkien ever wrote, if he had followed through on the impulse that led him to begin the *Narn i Chîn Húrin,* apparently in the early 1950s. Some of his very best work dates from that period, after *The Lord of the Rings* had been finished but before it reached print. As he wrote to Sir Stanley Unwin in 1950:

> For me the chief thing is that I feel the whole matter is now 'exorcized', and rides me no more. I can turn now to other things, such as perhaps the Little Kingdom of the Wormings, or to quite other matters and stories.

In the event, few of the tales he projected in those days were ever taken up, and none were finished; but before the impulse failed, he had written substantial chunks of a 'novelistic' retelling of *The Silmarillion*. That would have been worth having, and arguably it would have been a better use of Tolkien's time than the academic busywork that fretted him until his retirement in 1959. But it was not to be. Portions of it were cannibalized for Christopher Tolkien's 1977 edition of *The Silmarillion*, and much more for *Unfinished Tales* and the last four volumes in the *History of Middle-earth*. I understand that some still has not been published. *The Children of Húrin* represents Christopher Tolkien's best effort to present one of the 'late' long-form tales as a complete and independent story. It is an admirable effort, ennobled by his scrupulous refusal to add more than a few connective phrases to his father's unfinished and disjointed drafts. But at the same time it is essentially quixotic. The thing cannot be done; there is not enough of the raw material to do it with.

And not all the material that exists is really suitable in tone for readers expecting a modern novel. Many people complained because *The Silmarillion* begins with a creation myth, like the Old Testament. They will not be better pleased to find that *Children* begins with a genealogy, like the New:

> Hador Goldenhead was a lord of the Edain and well-beloved by the Eldar. He dwelt while his days lasted under the lordship of Fingolfin, who gave to him wide lands in that region of Hithlum which was called Dor-lómin. His daughter Glóredhel wedded Haldir son of Halmir, lord of the Men of Brethil; and at the same feast his son Galdor the Tall wedded Hareth, the daughter of Halmir.

Children is typeset with short lines and wide line-spacing, and it is somewhat misleading to say that this retailing of family trees goes on for two straight pages. The tighter typography of the old Unwin (and Houghton Mifflin) hardcovers would have fitted it in a page; but even that is too much for modern stomachs.

'But now the tale returns,' Tolkien (father or son) says at last, 'to Húrin and Huor in the days of their youth.' That would have been a better place to begin. The story of their fight against the Orcs, their rescue by the Eagles and their secret sojourn in the hidden city of Gondolin, makes a gripping little tale; it could with profit have been longer. It is there that the essentials of the background are spelt out: the age-long war of the Elves against Morgoth, the friendship, sometimes tense and wary, between Elves and Men, and the foreknowledge that Gondolin, for all its secrecy, would be merely the last realm to go down before Morgoth to inevitable defeat. A few pages later, the lame craftsman Sador says all that is needful about Hador, 'the old lord,' and his successors down to Húrin; and the stuff about the Men of Brethil and their marital entanglements could well have been left until Túrin arrived in Brethil to make the relevance of this information clear.

The mediaeval audience of the *Beowulf*-scop, or even of the *Gawain*-poet, liked to know in advance who all the *dramatis personae* were, and how everyone was related to everyone else, and expected these things to be important to the plot. Modern readers, brought up as atoms in a society that hardly knows what a family is, have no patience for it. Regrettable as this may be, it is pointless to burden them at the outset with knowledge that they do not know how to want.

The story really takes on detail and interest with the Black Breath and the death of Túrin's sister Lalaith, and gathers speed and force as Húrin rides to war in the host of King Fingon. The account of the Battle of Unnumbered Tears is grievously docked, according to Tolkien's own intention but, I suspect, much to the confusion of those who have not read the full account in Chapter 20 of *The Silmarillion*. The exact details of the eastern battle we can get by without; but more probably needs to be said about the Union of Maedhros, and about who Maedhros was and why his Union in fact failed to unite all the Elves of Beleriand. Few of the folk of Nargothrond joined his alliance, and hardly any from Doriath; and as those are the Elf-kingdoms principally dealt with in *Children,* it might have been helpful to explain why. The whole atmosphere of the tale is one of brooding fatality, of suspicion between friends, distrust and division between ancient allies; but if you were to read *Children* without having read *The Silmarillion*, that mood might seem strange and unmotivated. This was an avoidable lacuna, created perhaps by Christopher Tolkien's unwillingness to splice in bits of extraneous text or to venture explanations of his own.

A worse gap, but an unavoidable one, occurs in the very heart of the book, in Chapters XI and XII. Túrin's fate was foreshadowed from his childhood, but sealed by his rejection of Finduilas and her ill-starred love. This is glossed over in a few short passages, for Tolkien never wrote any long version of the Finduilas story. Christopher has included a fragment dealing with the love-triangle of Túrin, Finduilas and Gwindor, but not enough to build up its significance, or to carry the emotional weight that conditioned Túrin's later dealings with the unknown maiden who turned out to be his sister.

In a purely factual sense, however, enough is told to convey the story in essence. Tom Deveson misses the point, or perverts it wilfully to revive the old charge of racism against Tolkien:

> When, after a long separation, he meets and falls in love with his sister, she is "tall, and her eyes were blue, her hair fine gold" – now there's a surprise. Lineage is all and virtue is hereditary.

The people of Hador were of what we should describe as a Scandinavian type; they were nearly all tall, blue-eyed and fair-haired, Túrin himself being an exception because of his foreign mother. (The people of Bëor, from whom Morwen was descended, bear a decided resemblance to the Brythonic Celts, and the woodland people of Haleth to the Finns. Tolkien's taste in languages comes out in unexpected ways.) It hardly counts as racism to say that Niënor resembled most other people of her race. But Túrin's attraction to her does not depend merely upon the supposed bias of Western society in favour of leggy blondes. He has but lately learned the grisly circumstances of Finduilas's death, and regretted his failure to requite her love, when he finds this unknown maiden lying unconscious on Finduilas's burial-mound. If you have paid attention to the (all too brief) descriptions in the Nargothrond chapters, she appears to him almost as Finduilas returned to life:

> Finduilas the daughter of Orodreth found her heart moved whenever he came near, or was in hall. She was golden-haired after the manner of the house of Finarfin, and Túrin began to take pleasure in the sight of her and in her company; for she reminded him of his kindred and the women of Dor-lómin in his father's house.

When Túrin sees Niënor on the grave of Finduilas, the circle of memory is closed: for this is in truth a woman of his father's house. But because he has never met Niënor before, and has no reason to guess that she has left the safety of Doriath, he fails to recognize her, and that circle becomes a noose that soon draws tight around them both. In the end Glaurung the dragon reveals to Niënor that Turambar, her husband, is also Túrin, her brother. Believing that he is dead, she despairs of him, and knowing that she has committed incest, she despairs of herself for shame; and nothing short of suicide can allay her grief. Then Túrin in his turn finds out the truth and kills himself.

This is the crux of the tale, the element Tolkien took from the *Kalevala* and made his own. It is only the 'elvishness' of *The Children of Húrin*, its place in the high matter of the Elder Days, that raises it above the sordid tale of Kullervo. But to know this you would have to do some reading; you would need to know more about *The Silmarillion*, and about mythology in general, than a Deveson is allowed to know without surrendering his licence to sneer.

In like fashion, Ms. Salij aims an ignorant barb at Tolkien, or what she fondly believes to be a barb:

> Tolkien's weakness for making his heroes so very, very good and his villains so very, very bad is particularly grating. Middle-Earth is the place to go if you must have the morality of

your fiction be black and white, and apparently the simplicity
was worse early in its history.

Beyond any doubt Túrin is the protagonist of *Children,* and the hero of
the tale if it has one. He has the interesting trait, common enough among
'men of honour' in primitive cultures and still more in their mythological
traditions, of having the strictest scruples without any actual morals. He
is stubborn, stiff-necked, wilful, impulsive, violently touchy, immune to
good advice, and prone to murderous rages against his closest friends; I
can barely resist adding, 'And those are his good points.' I can account for
Ms. Salij's complaint in only two ways. Either she had already made up
her mind to complain about 'black and white morality' before ever reading the book, or she really does think that a near-psychopath like Túrin
is 'so very, very good.' I am not quite sure which explanation disturbs me
more.

Even the Elven-kings, Thingol and Orodreth, are reckless and pusil-
lanimous by turns, and push Túrin and his sister towards their grisly
doom by their foolish miscalculations. On the other side, Morgoth himself is Tolkien's Satan-figure, and not meant to be a sympathetic character
in any respect; for Tolkien knew what traps awaited him if he followed
too closely in the footsteps of Milton. But he is not a significant mover
in the plot. Everything that happens to Húrin's son and daughter is, as it
were, over-determined; in fact, the whole plot is a formidable inquisition
into the nature of fate and free will. We see it first in the description of
Túrin's friend Sador:

> He had been a woodman, and by ill-luck or the mishandling of
> his axe he had hewn his right foot. . . .

Which is it, fate or his own lack of skill? Is it Túrin's obsession with
Finduilas that leads him to commit incest with his sister, or the doom laid
upon them by Morgoth? Is it Morwen's pride that leads her to separate
herself from her son, and then abandon all safety to go chasing after him
when it is too late to save him? Or is some more elemental evil at work? In

Chapter V, Túrin himself leaves Doriath because he has chased Saeros to his death over an insult; as so often happens, Saeros's words struck a sorer spot than he intended. But between the insult and the revenge, Mablung the Hunter touches on the same question of fate versus freedom:

> 'But if either be slain it will be an evil deed, more fit for Angband than for Doriath, and more evil will come of it. Indeed I feel that some shadow of the North has reached out to touch us tonight. Take heed, Saeros, lest you do the will of Morgoth in your pride, and remember that you are of the Eldar.'

In the whole tragedy of Húrin and his family, the only character who acts in direct obedience to Morgoth is Glaurung. He pushes the plot along at crucial moments, first by diverting Túrin from Finduilas's trail, then by wiping out Niënor's memory, and in the end by restoring it before he dies; but these things, while necessary to accomplish Morgoth's vengeance, are far from sufficient. More important are the times when the human characters do Morgoth's will by their own free choice. The whole plot reminds me of the traps and temptations in *The Screwtape Letters,* with the epic *gravitas* of an ancient skald in place of Screwtape's corrosive wit.

What is the flaw in the world that makes all our paths turn crooked against our will; or in ourselves, that we choose the crooked path when we would walk straight? The question was old when Shakespeare made it the moral heart of *Macbeth,* and when it vexed St. Paul a millennium and a half before:

> For I know that in me (that is, in my flesh,) dwelleth no good thing: for to will is present with me; but how to perform that which is good I find not. For the good that I would I do not: but the evil which I would not, that I do.

Those verses would serve well as an epitaph for Túrin and his family. In *The Children of Húrin,* for all its flaws and gaps, Tolkien has produced a masterly meditation on the evil that lies sleeping in the human heart, and the evil in the world that calls it into wakefulness. Even in this incomplete form, it stands as a monument to the themes and obsessions that drove Tolkien to write the calamitous history of the Eldar.

Who, then, is morally simplistic, or childish, or escapist? Is it the great authors of the last century – Tolkien, Orwell, Vonnegut, Burgess, to name only a few – who dressed up human wickedness in fairy-tale costumes so that we could bear to look upon it and call it by its name? Or the academics and critics, the Modernists and Postmodernists, who refused to look and pretended it did not exist? It takes a peculiar and wilful blindness to accuse Tolkien of moral puerility, or to read him without seeing the deadly seriousness of the issues his fantasies raise. *The Children of Húrin* is Tolkien at his darkest, Tolkien looking into the abyss; and I find it deeply disturbing that none of his enemies and few of his friends seem capable of grasping the fact.

LOST TALES, UNATTAINED VISTAS

The fantasy boom of 1977 would never have happened without *The Lord of the Rings* to blaze the trail, and it probably would not have happened at that time but for the fever of anticipation for *The Silmarillion*. When that book finally appeared, four years after its author's death and forty years after it was first offered to a publisher, legions of fans rushed out to buy it, and thousands of them never finished it. I cannot think of any other instance in which an author engendered such high expectations for his next book, and produced a book so wildly incongruous with those expectations. It was as if a stadium full of people had come to see a football match, and were treated to an ice ballet instead.

In fiction, as in every art, nothing is more fatal to enjoyment than the tyranny of expectations. It is a common complaint among authors that their readers are always badgering them to write the same book again and again. Sometimes the authors resist this demand, sometimes they give in, as L. Frank Baum did, and grind out joyless sequels until the whole of the original inspiration is forgotten and only self-parody remains. Baum tried very hard not to write sequels to *The Wonderful Wizard of Oz*. He even proclaimed, at the end of one of the books, that Oz had been cut off for ever from communication with the outside world, and no more stories about it could possibly be told; but the children of America still pestered him for more, and he was slaving away at the fourteenth book when he died. Piers Anthony is probably the leading exponent of that school today, but there are scores of other unhappy offenders. Go to any bookshop with a well-stocked science fiction and fantasy section, and you will see more evidence than you could want. Instead of continuing to create original work, many an author has become merely the head writer of his own franchise, and his later books, in effect, are merely tie-ins to his early ones.

Tolkien escaped this treadmill by the clever expedient of being unable to tread it. He had never meant to write *The Lord of the Rings* in any case: his heart in the 1930s was with *The Silmarillion* and its natural sequel, the story of Númenor. It was Stanley Unwin (and a horde of eager children) who wanted a sequel to *The Hobbit,* and as you can see in the halting and erratic manuscripts collected in *The Return of the Shadow,* it puzzled Tolkien mightily to invent one. But he was determined to please, as determined as Bilbo:

> 'Tell me what you want done, and I will try it, if I have to walk
> from here to the East of East and fight the wild Were-worms in
> the Last Desert.'

But the fulfilment of that promise brought him to the very end of the impulse that began with the strange words, 'In a hole in the ground there lived a hobbit.' Tolkien had nothing more to say about the inhabitants of the Shire and their incongruous modern Englishry. He returned with joy (and vastly improved technique) to the matter of the Elder Days and of Númenor, and for a while, until power and hope began to fail him, he produced quantities of story as magnificent as anything he had yet published.

I say 'quantities of story', not 'stories', for in the event none of the new tales were ever finished. Fans were pressing for another book, and although they, being fans, wanted more of the same, he had anticipated and misdirected them, dotting his Appendices with references to something called *The Silmarillion.* Trusting rather naively that his intentions were congruent with theirs, the fans fixed all their hopes upon this mysterious book, and began to clamour specifically for that. But this left Tolkien in a cleft stick. *The Silmarillion* was nearly finished when he set it aside; it wanted only to be harmonized with *The Lord of the Rings.* That was not a simple task, but it could probably have been accomplished in a year or two if he had pursued it as his sole and fixed intention. But Tolkien's intentions were seldom fixed and never solitary. He was at his best when driving projects three or four abreast, following their demands and implications wherever they led, even to places wholly unexpected.

So he wrote part of *The Mariner's Wife,* and part of the *Narn i Chîn Húrin,* and made a fresh start on *The Lay of Leithian,* and had a go at *The Notion Club Papers,* and even tried coming up with a tale of the Fourth Age, *The New Shadow;* and he wrote long and involved explanations of the recondite details of Middle-earth in letters to fans, or in essays for his own reference (and amusement). But none of this brought him any nearer to his professed goal. Meanwhile he fell very much out of conceit with some of his most important early conceptions, as I have mentioned: he wanted to do away with the etiological myth of the Sun and Moon, and change the story of the origin of Men, and he never did come up with a satisfactory explanation of the Orcs. Matters like these, and the unending task of refining his invented languages, occupied him almost exclusively in his last years. In the end he died with a study full of chaotic and unfinished manuscripts, no closer to finishing *The Silmarillion* in 1973 than he had been in 1937.

In the circumstances, when *The Silmarillion* finally appeared, what could it have been but a fascinating and ambitious failure?

To every imaginative writer of genius, and to many of us who lack it, there comes a sort of climacteric at which the Secondary World ceases to grow and begins instead to ripen. Tolkien's climacteric seems to have come in 1943, when he made the map of Middle-earth in coloured chalks that was pinned above his desk ever after. From the small and tentative landfall of the 'Lost Tales', Middle-earth had grown into an impressive edifice, as big as Europe and nearly as diverse, weighted with three ages of history

WRITING DOWN THE DRAGON

and regret. It grew no more thereafter. There was never any map of Rhûn or Harad, nor a history of the Fourth Age beyond the reign of Eldarion. From then on he exerted himself to fill in the white spaces on the map, to bridge the gaps in the chronologies, to give narrative form and fullness to events only sketched in outline before.

Compared to the vast spaces of the 1943 map, and the 6,000-year span of *The Tale of Years*, the chronicle of the Elder Days was a little thing, just about a tenth as large in both space and time; and in the original *Book of Lost Tales* it was smaller still. But it was still too great in scope for a single novel. Stanley Unwin, though he wrote on the strength of such scanty information that he ought to have been ashamed to say anything at all, scored an accidental bull's-eye when he told Tolkien:

> *The Silmarillion* contains plenty of wonderful material; in fact it is a mine to be explored in writing further books like *The Hobbit* rather than a book in itself.

The original *Book of Lost Tales,* though still a mass of fragments when its author abandoned it, was already rather longer than the published *Quenta Silmarillion.* Still to be written were 'Gilfanon's Tale', which would have covered the whole period from the exile of the Noldoli (later Noldor) to the Battle of Unnumbered Tears, and the story of Eärendil, which was never written save in outline, though it was to be the climax of the whole work.

Much has been written about Tolkien's sources and influences, especially the sources of individual 'motifs' and plot-elements in his books. There is less discussion of his formal models, which is a great pity, because these give, in a sense, the key to the whole work. The single greatest influence on the 'Lost Tales' was of course the *Kalevala,* which was intended to be a comprehensive compilation of the heroic poetry of the Finns – though Tolkien's tales were in prose. The *Prose Edda* was a model, and quite a logical one, for the radical abridgement of the 'Lost Tales' which Tolkien composed (apparently from memory) for R.W. Reynolds. In both cases the prose work was a précis of the existing body of legend, provided as an aid to readers or students of the surviving poems and sagas, so that they could understand the names and allusions and place each work correctly in the context of the whole.

Of course not all Tolkien's influences were 'Northern', though those are naturally the ones most dwelt upon by biographizing critics. The earlier chapters of *The Book of Lost Tales* show the clear influence of the Old Testament, and 'The Music of the Ainur' (later *Ainulindalë*) is much closer to Genesis than to any pagan creation-myth. The middle part, from the making of the Silmarils to 'The Fall of Gondolin', bears a definite resemblance to the *Iliad*. Both are war-stories, of course, and in both it is much the same kind of war, a series of dramatically stylized battles and exploits, studded with heroes whose names were worth a thousand swords apiece, and incomprehensible without a fairly detailed knowledge of those heroes' ancestral feuds and motivations. Both stories are much easier reading (for us ignorant moderns) with the help of a large genealogical table. Then the war ends in catastrophe, and in its aftermath Tolkien and Homer go haring off to sea. The tale of Eärendil, as outlined, bears some comparison with the *Odyssey*, and also with the stories about Sinbad the Sailor. Tolkien cannot have cared much for the extravagances and crudities of *The Book of One Thousand and One Nights*, any more than for the Matter of Britain ('too lavish, and fantastical, incoherent and repetitive') or for Shakespeare's touches of fantasy in *Macbeth*. But Arthur and *Macbeth* left their imprint upon him, and I doubt that he wholly escaped the influence of the 'arabesque' fantasy so popular in his youth.

For the nineteenth century was a mythologizing age. What Lönnrot did for (or to) Finnish legend in the *Kalevala* was by no means unique. The Brothers Grimm set the fashion with their collection of German folk-tales. Sir Walter Scott and Thomas Percy did the same for the Scots and northern English, Lady Charlotte Guest for the Welsh (who scarcely needed her help), Schoolcraft and Longfellow for the Ojibwe, and so on. Macaulay even attempted something of the kind in his *Lays of Ancient Rome*. It was part of the new religion of nationalism that every great and civilized nation should have its own sacred myths. Even the French had one, though it was not a myth of the ancients, but of the moderns who cast off the shroud of barbarism and the yoke of feudalism in the glorious convulsion of 1789, and so created true civilization and the enlightenment of Man. This myth was largely put about by the French Revolutionaries themselves, but in spite of its obvious falsehoods it has its enthusiasts to this day.

But among all the proud nations with their myth-making clamour, there was one that held a curious silence; and that was England, the most powerful and influential nation of all. A sane mind might have suggested that so striking an exception invalidated the rule. But it takes uncommon insight and courage to be sane about the characteristic insanities of one's own time. Instead the Romantic theorists set to work to explain the exception, or explain it away. Some held that the English were not truly civilized, but merely a race of money-grubbing ogres in top hats who had got rather above themselves. Others suggested that the English had once had a mythological tradition as rich as anyone's, but had lost it in the cataclysm of the Norman Conquest. Tolkien made himself the champion of this latter school. In his academic work he strove to recapture and rehabilitate whatever survived of the stories of pre-Norman England, even the cryptic tales embedded in place-names; but in the work of his heart he tried another method entirely.

This method was not original with Tolkien, but he was perhaps the first to pursue it so industriously without nefarious intent. The 'Ossian' poems set a standard for this kind of literary deception, and indeed did much to engender interest in comparative or competitive mythology. In the nineteenth century, various authors invented or adapted myth-cycles to buttress their own invented religions. Any list of these would be controversial, and indeed grossly offensive to their present-day adherents, for several of these religions persist strongly. I will confine myself to saying that the accusation has been made against such persons as Joseph Smith, Mary Baker Eddy, and Madame Blavatsky.

Tolkien might well have hung a bogus religion on the framework of the 'Lost Tales', but he was well inoculated against that folly. For his romanticism was not dedicated to England only, but also to the Catholic Church. His approach to religion, unlike his friend Lewis's, was almost entirely emotional, founded in what he considered (not unfairly) to be his mother's martyrdom. Mabel Tolkien might well have died of her diabetes in any case, but not in such cold comfort, nor leaving her sons in such penury, had not both her family and her late husband's spurned her as a papist. When Tolkien's romantic spirit moved him to write fairy-stories, his conscience as a Catholic forbade him to pass them off as genuine private revelations, just as his conscience as a scholar in Old and Middle English forbade him to pass them off as genuine English legends. He therefore determined to offer them simply for what they were – a body of invented tales dedicated 'to England; to my country'.

So he told Milton Waldman in 1951, in an impassioned plea to have *The Silmarillion* published in conjunction with *The Lord of the Rings*. But in the bitter austerity of postwar Britain, with its devalued currency and strictly rationed paper, it was an impossible request. The England of Chaucer and Shakespeare would have delighted in Tolkien's gift; the England of Clement Attlee could not afford to accept it.

For a gift dedicated to England, *The Silmarillion* is remarkably un-English. Allen & Unwin's reader wrote, in a remark made infamous by Humphrey Carpenter's biography of Tolkien:

> It has something of that mad, bright-eyed beauty that perplexes
> all Anglo-Saxons in the face of Celtic art.

But this was wide of the mark. The exceedingly complicated web of Elvish histories and languages was in part Tolkien's attempt to make sense (and style) of the confusion of the Prose Edda, with its *ljosálfar, dökkálfar*, and *svartálfar*. The story of Túrin was frankly modelled after the tale of Kullervo in the *Kalevala*. Tolkien was deeply enamoured of the sound and structure of the Welsh language, but genuine Celtic legends left him cold. He agreed frankly that they were in fact 'mad', and was rather hurt to see *The Silmarillion* tarred with the same brush. In fact the Celtic influence on Tolkien's fiction was fairly small. But the uniquely English element (if we exception the brazen anachronism of the Hobbits) was smaller still.

But that exception is vital, for it was Hobbits that made it possible for *The Lord of the Rings* to succeed. Few modern Englishmen, and not many modern readers of any nationality, could easily identify with the heroic nihilism of Túrin or the romantic bravado of Beren, let alone with the high-minded loyalties and hatreds of the Elves. But almost anyone can identify with Bilbo, Frodo, or Sam. They mediate between the high style of archaic romance and the familiar conventions of the modern novel. Whatever *The Silmarillion* is, it is not a novel. Many of the constituent tales do not even descend to the level of romance, but breathe the cold and rarefied air of pure myth. What they lack is a landfall, a point of contact between the legendarium and the modern reader.

Tolkien felt this lack keenly, and tried many different ways to supply such a contact. The original 'Lost Tales' were told by various Elves to one Eriol or Ælfwine, an Anglo-Saxon mariner. This at any rate mediated between myth and early English history, but that is not much help to the average reader. To most of us, Ælfwine of England is almost as remote a figure as an Elvish king. Later, though he never quite gave up on Ælfwine, Tolkien made *The Silmarillion* a compendium of still older tales, prepared and abridged by an Elvish sage, Rúmil or Pengoloð. In The Lost Road and The Notion Club Papers, the tales of Númenor were conveyed to modern Englishmen in dreams and visions; this is one step better, but not a large step, for they were very curious and atypical Englishmen – almost as strange as Tolkien himself. It is very curious that he never settled upon the obvious method of relating *The Silmarillion* to the 'Red Book of Westmarch', by deriving it from Bilbo's three books of 'Translations from the Elvish'. That would at least have allowed him to introduce the legends in a familiar Hobbit-voice, and given us a firm imaginative vantage-point from which to look back at the history of the Elder Days.

But this was perhaps the lesser of two intractable problems. The other was the entire matter of style and presentation. As I have said, the original 'Lost Tales' were written at greater length than their counterparts in the finished *Silmarillion;* and much was lost in the abridgement. The cold and august style of Tolkien's last years had great poetic beauty, but it could not easily descend to everyday incidents and emotions. Like Treebeard, it was 'not very, hm, bendable'. The style of the 'Lost Tales' is quite different: occasionally twee (as in the dire frame-story, 'The Cottage of Lost Play'), sometimes grating as it reaches too hard for an archaic effect, but vivid and immediate, with an emotional palette ranging from bitter tragedy to low comedy. The strong sensuous detail that made *The Lord of the Rings* so compelling is just as pronounced in, for example, 'The Coming of the Elves'.

Here Ulmo has drawn the first two kindreds of the Eldar across the Sea to Valinor on a movable island; but Ossë, who in this version is a rather vain and puckish junior sea-god, does not want the third kindred to follow them and leave him lonely:

> Then Ossë seizes that island in his great hand, and all the great strength of Uin may scarcely drag it onward. . . . Now ere [Ulmo] can return Ossë with Ónen's aid had brought the isle to a stand, and was anchoring it even to the sea-bottom with giant ropes of those leather-weeds and polyps that in those dark days had grown already in slow centuries to unimagined girth about the pillars of his deep-sea house. Thereto as Ulmo urges the whales to put forth all their strength and himself aids with all his godlike power, Ossë piles rocks and boulders of huge mass that Melko's ancient wrath had strewn about the seafloor, and builds these as a column beneath the island.

The island is stuck fast and cannot make the third trip. But Ulmo has the last laugh, for he fetches the rest of the Elves across in ships, with a novel means of propulsion:

> Now does Aulë of the sawn wood of pine and oak make great vessels like to the bodies of swans, and these he covers with the bark of silver birches, or . . . with gathered feathers of the oily plumage of Ossë's birds, and they are nailed and riveted and fastened with silver, and he carves prows for them like the upheld necks of swans, but they are hollow and have no feet;

and by cords of great strength and slimness are gulls and petrels harnessed to them, for they were tame to the hands of the
Solosimpi, because their hearts were so turned by Ossë. . . .

Now all are embarked and the gulls fare mightily into the
twilit sky, but Aulë and Oromë are in the foremost galley and
the mightiest, and seven hundred gulls are harnessed thereto
and it gleams with silver and white feathers, and has a beak of
gold and eyes of jet and amber. But Ulmo fares at the rear in his
fishy car and trumpets loudly for the discomfiture of Ossë and
the rescue of the Shoreland Elves.

All this 'business' is lost in the mature *Silmarillion:*

Now Ossë followed after the host of Olwë, and when they were
come to the Bay of Eldamar (which is Elvenhome) he called
to them; and they knew his voice, and begged Ulmo to stay
their voyage. And Ulmo granted their request, and at his bid-
ding Ossë made fast the island and rooted it to the foundations
of the sea. Ulmo did this the more readily, for he understood
the hearts of the Teleri, and in the council of the Valar he had
spoken against the summons, thinking that it were better for
the Quendi to remain in Middle-earth. . . . But the island was
not moved again, and stood there alone in the Bay of Eldamar;
and it was called Tol Eressëa, the Lonely Isle.

Gone are the jet and amber, the gulls and petrels, the swan-bodied
ships of Aulë, and Ulmo's 'fishy car' (so clearly patterned upon Poseidon's
chariot). Gone, too, are the interesting dissensions among the Valar, for
Tolkien in his old age found such things impossible to reconcile with his
theological preoccupations. It is duller than the earlier story, for precisely
the same reason that Dante's *Paradiso* is duller than his *Inferno,* or that
Paradise Regained is duller than *Paradise Lost.* Or to take another example, distinctly lesser but perhaps more familiar, it is like the difference
between the original *Star Trek* and *Star Trek: The Next Generation.* The

second series was more polished and ambitious than the first, but when Gene Roddenberry laid down the law that there should be no inter-personal conflicts among the crew of the *Enterprise* D, much salt went out of the work. The friendly sparring of Spock and McCoy, or of Ulmo and Ossë, was an element that should not lightly have been lost.

But the heart of *The Silmarillion* is not in these early myths, but in the four great tales of Beren, Túrin, Tuor, and Eärendil, the heroic Men who fought desperately to prevent the final triumph of Morgoth. The tale of Eärendil was never written in full, and the tale of Tuor never rewritten after the very early and unsatisfactory 'Fall of Gondolin'; but the other two tales were recast and rewritten with almost manic fecundity. Tolkien never gave up trying to portray Beren and Túrin at full length, in prose or in verse. *The Lay of the Children of Húrin* is not a particularly effect-ive poem, and its 2,276 lines served chiefly to give the author practice in writing alliterative verse; but the much later *Narn i Chîn Húrin* is an un-finished masterpiece. With *The Children of Húrin,* after a lapse of seventy years, Christopher Tolkien took Unwin's advice and used *The Silmarillion* as 'a mine to be explored in writing further books'.

I think this was the correct decision, and one implicit in the nature of the material. *The Silmarillion* is, as I have said, not a novel, and even as an epic romance it is rather unsatisfactory. Some critics accuse it of lacking unity. Actually it has a powerful unity, but it is the unity appropriate to history rather than fiction. There is no principal character that we can fol-low through his adventures to discover that world, as we discovered the Middle-earth of the Third Age through Frodo and his friends. The heroes come and go – Fëanor, Fingolfin, Finrod, Maedhros, Haleth, Hador, Lúthien, and the rest – some tragic, some ambivalent, nearly all doomed – more heroes than some novels have characters, and each the centre of his own tale. Homer knew better: he focused the *Iliad* tightly on Hector and Achilles, and left most of the Matter of Troy aside. *The Silmarillion* should not have been an epic, even a prose epic, but a cycle of epics.

At one time, indeed, rumour said that it would be released in four volumes, and that might have been the better approach. A very successful version might have been constructed with one volume dedicated to each of the four great tales, and the earlier history of the Eldar and the Silmarils brought in gradually as backstory. The history of Fëanor would have been a logical annexe to the tale of Beren and Lúthien. The Valaquenta and the early wars of the Valar against Morgoth would have fitted well with the tale of Túrin, since 'in it are revealed most evil works of Morgoth Bauglir'. The story of the Nauglamír (or Nauglafring) was explicitly intended as the opening section of the Tale of Eärendil; and so on. Then each book would have had a sympathetic protagonist, and a hook upon which to hang a more or less novelistic structure; and they would also have retained some of the enchantment of remote vistas that Tolkien recognized to be so powerful an attraction in *The Lord of the Rings*:

> Part of the attraction of The L. R. is, I think, due to the glimpses of a large history in the background: an attraction like that of viewing far off an unvisited island, or seeing the towers of a distant city gleaming in a sunlit mist. To go there is to destroy the magic, unless new unattainable vistas are again revealed.

Macaulay's Roman poems strove after such an effect, as Tom Shippey describes in *Author of the Century*:

> People learned to read histories and historical poems with a kind of double vision, to see both the event being described and the context in which it was described. Macaulay built this kind of vision into 'Horatius' . . . by including evidently nostalgic remarks about 'the brave days of old', which show that his feigned 'lay' is deliberately looking backward from some historical distance. It has two dates in it, event, and record. This is the kind of thing flattened out by the treatments of Virgil or Livy.

And it is, alas, flattened out by the treatment of *The Silmarillion*. The ingredients are there for a headier potion even than *The Lord of the Rings* itself: Bilbo, translating from the Elvish at a remove of six thousand years, looking back upon Túrin Turambar, who himself looks back in awe and wonder at the abyss of ages before the Sun and Moon were made. And Bilbo himself, though a comparatively homely figure, has a sufficient air of 'long ago and far away' to lend him some of that same glamour. It would be a triple dose in place of Macaulay's double. To me, the most moving, indeed heartbreaking, line in *The Lord of the Rings* comes in Appendix A, at the end of 'a part of the tale of Aragorn and Arwen':

> Here ends this tale, as it has come to us from the South; and with the passing of Evenstar no more is said in this book of the days of old.

Already, when the Red Book of Westmarch took its final form, Aragorn and Arwen had passed into history, and their deaths were in 'the days of old'. It heightens still further the poignant sense of loss that hangs over *The Lord of the Rings* as a whole, and to me at least, makes it almost unbearable. It reminds us that the vista we have just seen is truly unattainable. Most fiction leaves us psychologically at the end of the principal action, looking forward in our imagination to the characters' future. Tolkien takes that away from us, reminding us again and again that even victorious heroes die, and are forgotten in the depths of time.

The story of *The Silmarillion*, then, is exceptionally well developed, but the treatment, as compressed into a single book without evident source or standpoint in the history of Middle-earth, is far inferior to what it could have been. Tolkien meant to do better, but he lost the main stream of the work in side-channels of history and theology, and his imagination ran dry in its own delta.

The Lord of the Rings was immensely successful, and has been endlessly imitated. *The Silmarillion,* which I believe had the potential to exceed that success, fell sadly short of its author's ambition, and has scarcely been imitated at all. I consider that one of the great tragedies of modern fantasy. A dwarf on a giant's shoulders sees further of the two: that is an old and commonplace saying. No one will ever write another *Lord of the Rings,* and it is high time that well-meaning fools gave up trying. But the work that Tolkien left unfinished is still worth attempting, and he came close enough that a dwarf on his shoulders might see the un-reached goal.

I do not mean that a lesser writer should try to fill the gaps in *The Silmarillion:* God forbid. What I mean is that it, rather than the much-abused *Lord of the Rings,* should provide a standard and a signpost, point-ing the way forward for epic fantasy. The Road goes ever on, but few have cared to follow it so far. If we truly honour the work of Tolkien's heart, we should be out there, blazing trails beyond the last milestone, seeking our way to vistas yet unattained.

WORKS CITED

1. Works of J. R. R. Tolkien

The principal sources for this work are, of course, the works of J. R. R. Tolkien himself. Of particular interest are the twelve volumes of the *History of Middle-earth*, which contain an immense quantity of Tolkien's early drafts, unpublished writings, private essays, and alternative readings of the published texts. The two-volume *History of the Hobbit*, edited by John D. Rateliff, is of great value in the study of *The Hobbit*.

There are now so many different editions of Tolkien's books, from different publishers and with different page-numbering, that it would be futile to give references by page number. Accordingly, I have chosen to give references by book and chapter, or (in the case of the *Letters*) by the number of the letter cited.

What follows is a partial list of Tolkien's works, including all those directly cited in this volume:

The Lord of the Rings: Originally (and still usually) published in three volumes:
The Fellowship of the Ring. London: George Allen & Unwin, 1954; 2nd ed., 1966.
The Two Towers. London: George Allen & Unwin, 1954; 2nd ed., 1966.
The Return of the King. London: George Allen & Unwin, 1955.

The Children of Húrin. London: HarperCollins, 2007.

Farmer Giles of Ham. London: George Allen & Unwin, 1949.

The Hobbit. London: George Allen & Unwin, 1937; 2nd ed., 1950.

The Letters of J. R. R. Tolkien. London: George Allen & Unwin, 1981.

The Silmarillion. Edited by Christopher Tolkien. London: George Allen & Unwin, 1977.

Tree and Leaf. 3rd ed. London: HarperCollins, 2001.

Unfinished Tales of Númenor and Middle-earth. London: George Allen & Unwin, 1980.

The History of Middle-earth: 12 volumes, edited by Christopher Tolkien, as follows:

1. *The Book of Lost Tales, Part I.* London: George Allen & Unwin, 1983.

2. *The Book of Lost Tales, Part II.* London: George Allen & Unwin, 1984.

3. *The Lays of Beleriand.* London: George Allen & Unwin, 1985.

4. *The Shaping of Middle-earth.* London: George Allen & Unwin, 1986.

5. *The Lost Road and Other Writings.* London: Unwin Hyman, 1987.

6. *The Return of the Shadow.* London: Unwin Hyman, 1988.

7. *The Treason of Isengard.* London: Unwin Hyman, 1989.

8. *The War of the Ring.* London: Unwin Hyman, 1990.

9. *Sauron Defeated.* London: HarperCollins, 1992.

10. *Morgoth's Ring.* London: HarperCollins, 1993.

11. *The War of the Jewels.* London: HarperCollins, 1994.

12. *The Peoples of Middle-earth.* London: HarperCollins, 1996.

2. Other sources

The literature of 'Tolkien Studies' is exceedingly voluminous, and increasing daily at an alarming rate. Fortunately, perhaps, the great majority of it is not suitable for the kind of limited study I have undertaken here – the study of Tolkien's writing methods from the perspective of a working fantasy writer. The most valuable sources I have found, by far, are Tom Shippey's *The Road to Middle-earth* and *J. R. R. Tolkien: Author of the Century.*

As with Tolkien's works, I give references by book and chapter. Many of these sources are available in electronic editions, either online or in ebook form, for which page numbers would be entirely unhelpful.

Alexander, Samuel. *Space, Time, and Deity.* London: Macmillan, 1920.
Aristotle. *Poetics.* Many translations and editions. Online at Project Gutenberg: http://www.gutenberg.org/ebooks/1974
Carpenter, Humphrey. *J. R. R. Tolkien: a biography.* London: George Allen & Unwin, 1977.
Clarke, Susanna. *Jonathan Strange and Mr. Norrell.* London: Bloomsbury, 2004.
Deveson, Tom. 'Away with the fairies'. *The Sunday Times,* 15 April 2007.
Donaldson, Stephen R. *The Real Story.* New York: Bantam, 1991.
Frye, Northrop. *Anatomy of Criticism: Four Essays.* Princeton: Princeton University Press, 1957.
Golding, William. *The Hot Gates.* London: Faber & Faber, 1965.
Helms, Randel. *Tolkien's World.* Boston: Houghton Mifflin, 1974.
Jones, Diana Wynne. *The Tough Guide to Fantasyland.* London: Vista, 1996.
Jones, Leslie. *J. R. R. Tolkien: A Biography.* Westport: Greenwood, 2003.
Le Guin, Ursula K. *The Language of the Night.* New York: G. P. Putnam's Sons, 1979.
Lewis, C. S. *Christian Reflections.* Cambridge: William B. Eerdmans, 1967. 'Fern-Seed and Elephants' is online: http://orthodox-web.tripod.com/papers/fern_seed.html
Lewis, C. S. *Out of the Silent Planet.* London: John Lane, The Bodley Head, 1938.
Moorcock, Michael. 'Wit and Humour in Fantasy'. *Foundation,* no. 16 (May 1979).
Myers, B. R. *A Reader's Manifesto.* New York: Melville House, 2002. An abridged version is online: http://www.theatlantic.com/magazine/archive/2001/07/a-readers-manifesto/302270/
Nielsen, Hans Frede. *The Germanic Languages: Origins and Early Dialectical Interrelations.* Tuscaloosa: University of Alabama Press, 1989.
Orwell, George. 'Good Bad Books'. *Tribune,* 2 November 1945. Online at http://www.george-orwell.org/Good_Bad_Books/0.html

Orwell, George. *Inside the Whale and Other Essays.* London: Gollancz, 1940. Title essay online at http://orwell.ru/library/essays/whale/english/e_itw

Orwell, George. 'Lear, Tolstoy, and the Fool'. *Polemic,* no. 7 (March 1947). Online at http://www.george-orwell.org/Lear,_Tolstoy_and_the_Fool/0.html

Peake, Mervyn. *Titus Alone.* London: Eyre and Spottiswoode, 1959.

Pohl, Frederik. *The Way the Future Was.* New York: Del Rey, 1978.

Salij, Marta. 'Just kick the hobbit and don't suffer "The Children of Hurin"'. *Detroit Free Press,* 18 April 2007.

Shippey, Tom. *J. R. R. Tolkien: Author of the Century.* London: HarperCollins, 2000.

Shippey, Tom. *The Road to Middle-earth.* 3rd ed. London: HarperCollins, 2003.

Twain, Mark. *The Adventures of Huckleberry Finn.* New York: Charles L. Webster, 1885. Online at Project Gutenberg: http://www.gutenberg.org/ebooks/76

Twain, Mark. *A Connecticut Yankee in King Arthur's Court.* New York: Charles L. Webster, 1889. Online at Project Gutenberg: http://www.gutenberg.org/ebooks/86

Twain, Mark. *Life on the Mississippi.* Boston: James R. Osgood & Company, 1883. Online at Project Gutenberg: http://www.gutenberg.org/ebooks/245

Williams, Charles. *Taliessin Through Logres.* Oxford: Oxford University Press, 1948.

Anonymous. *The Battle of Maldon.* Composed c. 1000. Original text: http://www8.georgetown.edu/departments/medieval/labyrinth/library/oe/texts/a9.html Modern English translation by Jonathan A. Glenn (1982): http://www.lightspill.com/poetry/oe/maldon.html

3. Specific references by chapter

In the following notes, all sources cited are by J. R. R. Tolkien unless otherwise specified.

The Riddles of the Wise

'Of this two things are said': *Unfinished Tales,*
'Ruddy little ignoramus': *Letters,* no. 45.

'Green great dragon': *Letters*, no. 163.

'Animalic' and 'Nevbosh': Carpenter, part II, chapter 3.

History of the Germanic dialects: Nielsen, *passim*.

'He hadn't ought to have went': Twain, *Life on the Mississippi*, chapter 44.

'Ond' meaning 'stone': *Letters*, no. 324.

'Nasc' as a 'short, hard, and clear vocable': *Letters*, no. 297.

For the history of philologists' attempts to analyse 'Hey diddle diddle', see Helms, chapter 7.

The Tolkien Method

The 'Sketch of the Mythology' and the *Quenta Noldorinwa* are printed in full in *The Shaping of Middle-earth*.

On Hobbits, Gollum, and birthday presents: *Letters*, no. 214.

Relation of 'hobbit' to 'Babbitt': Carpenter, part IV, chapter 6.

'Hobbit' not derived from 'Hobberdy Dick': *Letters*, no. 319.

'Cats of Queen Berúthiel': *The Fellowship of the Ring*, book II, chapter 4. The story linking her with King Tarannon is from *Unfinished Tales*, 'The Istari', note 7.

The Rhetoric of Middle-earth

'These men ask me to believe': Lewis, 'Fern-Seed and Elephants', reprinted in *Christian Reflections*.

'Enjoyment' and 'Contemplation': Alexander, *Space, Time, and Deity*.

'Sentence cult': Myers, *A Reader's Manifesto*.

'Good bad books': see Orwell's essay so titled.

Definitions of melodrama *vs.* drama: Donaldson, *The Real Story*, Afterword.

'The story is really a story of what happened': *Letters*, no. 186.

LOTR compared to *Boys Own Paper*: Referred to in *Letters*, no. 149.

'More or less a Warwickshire village': *Letters*, no. 178.

'Conceived in 1917 or thereabouts, Bertie': Orwell, 'In Defence of P. G. Wode-house'.

'Tim Benzedrine': Beard & Kenney, *Bored of the Rings*, chapter 2.

'Polders' & 'Thinning': Articles so titled in Clute & Grant, *Encyclopaedia of Fantasy*.

Romantic, ironic, and mimetic modes in fiction: Frye, *Anatomy of Criticism*.
Elrond as an ineffective chairman at the Council: Shippey, *Author of the Century*, chapter II.
'Fool of a Took!': *Fellowship of the Ring*, book II, chapter 4.
'Fool! Take it off! Take off the Ring!': *Fellowship*, book II, chapter 10.
'Nay, Gandalf!' and 'Not at all my dear G': *Letters*, no. 171.
'Orcs and Trolls spoke as they would': *The Return of the King*, Appendix F.
'Farewell, my hobbits!': *The Two Towers*, book III, chapter 8.
'Sam hesitated for a moment': *The Two Towers*, book IV, chapter 5.

Frodo's Vaunt
'For this "northern heroic spirit" is never quite pure': *Tree and Leaf*, 'Ofermod'.
'Ða se eorl ongan': *The Battle of Maldon*.
'Yet he does not rid himself of his chivalry': *Tree and Leaf*, 'Ofermod'.
'I am Aragorn son of Arathorn': *Fellowship of the Ring*, book I, chapter 10.
'Alas! Aragorn my friend!': *The Return of the King*, book V, chapter 2.
'They love their horses next to their kin': *The Fellowship of the Ring*, book II, chapter 2.
'It would be the death of you to come with me': Ibid., book II, chapter 10.
'It is but a trifle that Sauron fancies': Ibid., book II, chapter 2.
'Bilbo the silly hobbit started this': Ibid.
'I will take the Ring': Ibid.

The Method and the Morgoth
'So drastic was the revision': *Morgoth's Ring*, part I, 'Ainulindalë'.
'At that point… I was inclined to adhere to the Flat Earth': *Morgoth's Ring*, part 5, section I.
'[A] fearful weapon against his own creation': Ibid. (editorial note by Christopher Tolkien).
Athrabeth Finrod ah Andreth: *Morgoth's Ring*, part 4.

What Is Elf?
'There are no songs or stories preserved about Elves': *Letters*, no. 236.
'Goblin Feet': Quoted in Carpenter, part II, chapter 7.

'O! What are you doing': *The Hobbit,* chapter 3.
'"Elves" is a translation': *Letters,* no. 144.
'Now "Faërian Drama"': *Tree and Leaf,* 'On Fairy-stories'.
'This art of Enchantment': Ibid.
'Elves appear to have deteriorated': Jones, *The Tough Guide to Fantasyland,* entry 'Elves'.
'Gentleman with the Thistledown Hair': Clarke, *Jonathan Strange, passim.*
'Weston accepted the arrangement at once': Lewis, *Out of the Silent Planet,* chapter 20.
Perfect autocracy the best form of government: Twain, *A Connecticut Yankee,* chapter 10.
'The humans are always putting up claims': Lewis, *The Screwtape Letters,* chapter 21.

The Terminal Orc
'You might as well try to influence a Bandersnatch': C. S. Lewis, quoted in Jones, *J. R. R. Tolkien: A Biography,* 72.
Lewis's criticism of *The Lay of Leithian* and Tolkien's revisions: *The Lays of Beleriand,* part III, Appendix.
'Treebeard does not say that the Dark Lord "created"': *Letters,* no. 153.
'I must say that anyone who passed through those years': Golding, *The Hot Gates,* 'Fable'.
'Our eyes are directed to Rome': Orwell, *Inside the Whale,* 'Inside the Whale', part II.
'It's my guess you won't find much in that little fellow': *The Two Towers,* book IV, chapter 10.
'She's got more than one poison': Ibid.
'What can one say but "regular orcish trick"?': Shippey, *Author of the Century,* chapter 3.
'My dear tender little fools': *The Two Towers,* book III, chapter 3.
'I might not... have used the expression *poor little blighter*': *Letters,* no. 153.
'When he got out the new judge said he was a-going to make a man of him': Twain, *Huckleberry Finn,* chapter 5.

Writing Down the Dragon

'[A] little blind Oyarsa': Lewis, *Out of the Silent Planet,* chapter 20.

'Then pity rose in Túrin's heart': *The Silmarillion,* chapter 21.

'Glaurung spoke again': Ibid.

'[D]ragon-slayings historical, dubious, and mythical': *The Hobbit,* chapter 12.

'Dragons may not have much real use for all their wealth': Ibid.

'You have nice manners for a thief and a liar': Ibid.

'I suppose you got a fair price': Ibid.

Sauron not derived from *sauros: Letters,* no. 297. For the form *Thû,* see especially *The Shaping of Middle-earth.*

Moorcock, Saruman, and the Dragon's Tail

'Fritz Leiber and Roger Zelazny': Le Guin, *The Language of the Night,* 'From Elf-land to Poughkeepsie'.

'A new Power is rising': *The Fellowship of the Ring,* book II, chapter 2.

'The Magistrate leaned forward': *Titus Alone,* chapter 37.

'But more news came in': *Farmer Giles of Ham.*

The Abyss and the Critics

'Turin is captivated': Deveson, 'Away with the fairies'.

'Real archaic English is far more *terse*': *Letters,* no. 171.

'For me the chief thing': *Letters,* no. 124.

'When, after a long separation': Deveson, op. cit.

'Finduilas the daughter of Orodreth': *The Children of Húrin,* chapter 10.

'Tolkien's weakness for making his heroes so very, very good': Salij, 'Just kick the hobbit'.

'He had been a woodman': *The Children of Húrin,* chapter 1.

'But if either be slain it will be an evil deed': *The Children of Húrin,* chapter 5.

'For I know that in me... dwelleth no good thing': Romans 7:18–19.

Lost Tales, Unattained Vistas

'Tell me what you want done': *The Hobbit,* chapter 1.

'*The Silmarillion* contains plenty of wonderful material': Stanley Unwin, quoted in *The Lays of Beleriand*, 'Note on the original submission of the *Lay of Leithian* and *The Silmarillion* in 1937'.

'It has something of that mad, bright-eyed beauty': Reader's report on *The Silmarillion* to Stanley Unwin, 1937; quoted in Carpenter, *J. R. R. Tolkien: a biography*, part V, chapter 2.

'Then Ossë seizes that island': *The Book of Lost Tales, Part I*, chapter 5.

'Now does Aulë of the sawn wood': Ibid.

'Now Ossë followed after the host of Olwë': *The Silmarillion*, chapter 5.

'Part of the attraction of the L. R.': *Letters*, no. 247.

'People learned to read histories': Shippey, *Author of the Century*, chapter 5.

'Here ends this tale': *The Return of the King*, Appendix A.

ABOUT THE AUTHOR

Tom Simon discovered the world of J. R. R. Tolkien at the age of ten, when his teacher read *The Hobbit* aloud to her class. Two years later, his father gave him a boxed set of *The Lord of the Rings* as a Christmas present; but he filched it from his father's desk drawer and read about half of it before Christmas Day. Since then he has taken up writing epic fantasies of his own, including *Lord Talon's Revenge* and *The End of Earth and Sky,* both published as ebooks in 2012.

We invite you to visit Tom Simon's website at
bondwine.com

www.ingramcontent.com/pod-product-compliance
Lightning Source LLC
Chambersburg PA
CBHW030104070426
42448CB00037B/965